# Keeping Our Republic

# Keeping Our Republic

*Principles for a Political Reformation*

MATTHEW T. PARKS
AND
C. DAVID CORBIN

RESOURCE *Publications* • Eugene, Oregon

KEEPING OUR REPUBLIC
Principles for a Political Reformation

Resource Publications
An Imprint of Wipf and Stock Publishers
199 W. 8th Ave., Suite 3
Eugene, OR 97401
www.wipfandstock.com

ISBN 13: 978-1-61097-028-0

Manufactured in the U.S.A.

*To Rachel & Catie*

*"A republic, if you can keep it"*

—BENJAMIN FRANKLIN

# Contents

# Acknowledgments

W<small>E SHARE</small> a common intellectual debt to our great teacher, Angelo Codevilla, whose stamp can be found on all that is good in this short book. From our days as graduate students at Boston University to the development of this work, his wisdom and critical eye have challenged and shaped us. Our families have graciously encouraged and supported us during the progress of this project and have our deepest gratitude, love, and thanks. We are also very grateful for the careful work of our excellent copyeditor, Kristin Magee, and the team at Wipf and Stock that has shepherded us through this process.

# Introduction

*"If we could first know where we are, and whither we are tend-*
*ing, we could better judge what to do, and how to do it."*

–Abraham Lincoln,
"A House Divided," June 16, 1858

There is something wrong with our politics that elections
cannot solve. In recent years, we have had a Republican
Congress with a Democratic president, a Republican Congress
with a Republican president, a Democratic Congress with
a Republican president and a Democratic Congress with a
Democratic president. The "New Democrat" of 1992 produced a "Republican Revolution" in 1994. We cleansed ourselves of Clinton Administration corruption in 2000 only to
have to punish Republican corruption in 2006. "Hope and
Change" triumphed in 2008, while "Change That Matters"
flopped in 2010. For nearly twenty years, the American people have tried to mind their own business at home while car-
rying on a seemingly futile search for the right combination
of R's and D's in Washington. That search will not end until
we address the root of our political disorder: the progressive
abandonment of our republican principles and heritage.
Only a political reformation, calling us back to the wisdom
of our fathers and the founding documents of our nation, can
truly free us from the deeply-entrenched, bipartisan ruling
class that is bankrupting and degrading us. Only a political

reformation can "secure the Blessings of Liberty to ourselves *and* our Posterity . . . ."

## "WHERE WE ARE
## AND WHITHER WE ARE TENDING"

President Obama's administration has dramatically accelerated trends that have generally defined the politics of the last two decades: spending and deficits beyond all reasonable levels, expanded government control of our lives and livelihoods, and a growing disconnect between our privileged ruling class and the rest of America. The result has been an increasingly-disillusioned public and a consensus among "informed" commentators that we the people are too simple to deal with our complex problems, that the United States is in irreversible decline, and that only a rapid infusion of Chinese-style authoritarianism can stave off total collapse.

We believe that American decline is neither inevitable nor impossible. The rugged republican path by which thirteen New World colonies became history's freest, most prosperous, and most powerful nation remains open, though years of neglect may have allowed the wild undergrowth to the right and to the left to obscure the way. Clearing this path for use in our own generation must begin with a restatement of the key principles that have shaped it and a demonstration of their continued power to answer the needs of our time.

If reading or writing a book seems too slow a route to reformation, consider: it was *Common Sense* that moved the American colonists to action and *The Federalist Papers* that defined the core principles of our regime for generations. Many years later, the Reagan Revolution began with Barry Goldwater's *The Conscience of a Conservative*. Our own little contribution to the restoration of our republic, pygmies though we are among these giants, is grounded in the belief that we cannot break our cycle of electoral disappointments until we understand our political heritage and see clearly both "*where* we are and *whither* we are tending."

Anyone who looks into what ails us understands that the people who are making things worse believe that they are better than we are and know more than we know—and, therefore, that they are our natural rulers. To speak and act usefully, we have to be clear about why and how they are wrong. We have to be clear about what is right and why it is so. America's Founders also had to deal with rulers who assumed that they had a natural right to command. Our Founders were able to free themselves from their presumed betters because they tempered their anger with understanding and married theory to practice.

These early American statesmen knew what they wanted to create: as John Adams defined it (quoting Harrington), "an empire of laws, and not of men." In the best republic, the laws are made, executed, and enforced impartially, transparently, and exactly. Regardless of party or ideological affiliation, one could not claim that American government operates in such a manner today. This is not because we explicitly reject these ideals: every new politician enters office promising impartiality, transparency, and fair dealing. And yet far too often he becomes just one more leader quickly and quietly convinced that it is more convenient and desirable to use his office to reward friends and aggrandize himself.

## Republican and Post-Republican Citizens

Still, if our leaders have too often let us down, we must admit that central to our trouble is the fact that *we* have lost touch with what it means to be a *citizen* of a republic—to expect and demand nothing less and nothing more than the impartial, transparent, and exact administration of the law. Such a view of citizenship begins with an understanding of two fundamental moral facts about human beings: that we are equal in dignity with one another and morally responsible for the justice of our actions. Neither of these principles predetermines the right level of taxation or spending, the best measures for health care reform, or the particular policy to be adopted in any other area. They go deeper—to the very foundation of our political order. They demand of us: Have I proposed a rule for others that I could live with myself? Can I give a reason for my policy more meaningful than: "because I (or we) say so?"

We are not surprised to find, in contemporary America or anywhere else, that there are profound and seemingly intractable differences in how we answer the most basic political and philosophical questions. A republican citizen, however, recognizes that, as he pursues his own best understanding of the good life, there is no reason why either he or his neighbor, whatever their differences, should be denied the protection of his person and property—and no justification for making the terms of such protection more agreeable to those with power than those without it. Nevertheless, interest groups today cultivate division, appealing to our lowest desires for easy gain, and willingly subvert (and convince us to subvert) legitimate republican government for the sake of a merely private good. Of course, once the scrum begins, few can afford to be bystanders—or avoid the bruises to their dignity and mud stains on their character that inevitably follow. The result is something very different from the citizen of a republic—a thoroughly debased confidence man with a gift for rationalizing plunder.

## Republican and Post-Republican Statesmen

There is also a sort of political leadership suitable to a republic. A republican statesman respects the rule of law—he would not enslave free men even to free slaves. He would not take from Peter to give to Paul (or Mary). He leads as he would wish to be led. He doesn't play the part of the biased judge, the dictatorial executive, or the backroom legislator. His ambition is tied to upholding the empire of laws rather than furthering his empire over men.

Again, we are not surprised to find that many political leaders fall short of this mark. All humans seek recognition at some level. The most ambitious in our democratic age often possess a "fortunate astuteness" that enables them to take advantage of the many by convincing them that impartial, exact, and transparent governance is both unfeasible and undesirable. The history of our republic, however, tells a different tale. We need not hopelessly romanticize the past to know that there have been times when a greater regard for the common good prevailed among our leaders—or to see the blessings that resulted.

Post-republican American politicians come in all shapes and sizes. The great majority are office-seekers and -keepers. A smaller segment is made up of demagogues, living off and for the adulation of the crowd. The least typical and most dangerous of all are the would-be Caesars who would destroy our republic in their egomaniacal quest for individual glory. The alternative, in different ways, to each of these is the republican statesmen whose ambition is satisfied by the good work of preserving and purifying the regime.

## Republican and Post-Republican Politics

Although the American Founders understood that there was something decisively new in their approach to politics, they had no illusions that they had stumbled upon a new race of men, capable of transcending differences of opinion or interest. They themselves were often divided on important questions. Nevertheless, they recognized the distinction between divisions based upon competing understanding of what would serve the good of all and divisions arising out of the pursuit of merely private gain. While parties might legitimately result from the former, the latter could only be the source of special interest factions. Such groups deserved to be shamed and harried from the public square to whatever degree possible. So, while the Founders designed a Constitution that would make it difficult for special interest plots to succeed, they also stressed the moral dimension of political action: the reality of justice and the necessity of pursuing it lawfully and prudently.

We see precious little of this approach today. Instead of utilizing republican means, advocates for "change" (usually progressives) employ judicial fiat, the expansion of administrative rules and oversight, and an ever-growing body of entitlement legislation to achieve their vision of a just society. In such an environment, claims for justice are reduced to "might makes right," the law is something to be overcome rather than upheld, and prudence makes way for reckless experimentation or feckless appeasement.

## "WHAT TO DO AND HOW TO DO IT"

"*Where* we are" is a post-republican regime and "*whither* we are tending" is an even farther distance from republican citizenship, statesmanship, and politics. "*What* to do" is a matter of reviving republican habits in all three areas of our political life. If we can understand republican citizenship, statesmanship, and politics, we can work toward making the impartial, exact, and transparent administration of law the "generative fact" of American politics in theory and practice once again.

This short book hopes to contribute to this project by stating in precise terms what republican citizenship, statecraft, and politics are (and are not) in six concise chapters on equality, responsibility, honor, justice, lawfulness, and prudence, applied to the politics of our day. We believe that the revitalization of the American regime depends upon the revitalization of our common ability to tell the republican from the unrepublican as easily as we distinguish a Democrat from a Republican—and to recognize that the former skill is vastly more important than the latter.

Perhaps never before have the American people had before them such a clear alternative to their republican heritage—leaders who govern like lords, rather than servants, acting beyond the limits of law and custom in league with political allies and access-seekers, with the explicit aim of permanently transforming our political and social order. The resulting public discontent is broad and deep. And yet, while it has generated gut-level disgust with deficit spending, special interest politics, and state-run enterprise, it also needs a carefully-defined, principled alternative. This alternative, we believe, is the republicanism of Abraham Lincoln and the American Founders.

Our goal is not to promote the cause of one party or ideology, but to make the case for the re-establishment of an American empire of laws. If you are a Democrat, be a republican Democrat—like Thomas Jefferson. If you are a Republican, be a republican Republican—like Abraham Lincoln. If you are conservative, be a republican conservative—like George Washington. And if you are a liberal, be a republican liberal—like James Madison.

Keeping our republic is not a spectator sport but a grave contest that necessitates that we relearn how to think and how to act like republicans. It is our hope that this work will help equip you for that fight.

# 1

# Equality

*"As I would not be a slave, so I would not be a master."*

—ABRAHAM LINCOLN,
"FRAGMENT ON SLAVERY," AUGUST 1, 1858

FOR MORE than a generation, the medical choices of those over sixty-five have been largely controlled by the federal government, which has imposed payroll taxes on all and then decided for what and for whose care that money would be spent. Our contemporary health care debate amounts to a discussion of whether the medical choices of all Americans will be controlled in a similar way. And while the discussion in Washington has been about taxes and spending, the American public has been asking a more fundamental question: "Do we really want panels of 'experts' setting the rules by which we live and die?" When Sarah Palin crystallized the concern of millions by speaking out, somewhat provocatively, against "death panels," the response of the ruling class was scorn—nothing in their proposals would authorize anyone to sentence anyone else to death. But consider: Any government board that is responsible for deciding what medical procedures will be

1

allowed for which class of patients exists precisely to deny life-saving care to some (from whom the government has taken money they might have used to care for themselves) in order to grant it to others deemed to be more worthy. This is true all the more when the central mandate of such boards is to guarantee that health care spending goes down.

Despite its scorn, our ruling class does not really deny that it means to take life and death decisions into its own hands. In an interview with a *New York Times* reporter, President Obama spoke frankly about the fact that as much as 80 percent of the "total health care bill out there" comes from the "chronically ill and those toward the end of their lives." In response to the reporter's follow-up—"So how do you—how do we deal with it?"—the President made it clear that this was a matter for the experts: "Well, I think that there is going to have to be a conversation that is guided by doctors, scientists, ethicists. And then there is going to have to be a very difficult democratic conversation that takes place. It is very difficult to imagine the country making those decisions just through the normal political channels. And that's part of why you have to have some independent group that can give you guidance. It's not determinative, but I think has to be able to give you some guidance. And that's part of what I suspect you'll see emerging out of the various health care conversations that are taking place on the Hill right now."

Notice who is supposed to lead the "conversation" on the matter (i.e. the writing of countless pages of binding rules): "doctors, scientists, ethicists"—the sovereigns (with the politicians who appoint them) of our post-republican regime. Why do they get to decide how best to keep the chronically ill and elderly from running up the national "health care bill?" Because our ruling class thinks that it is entitled to rule its inferiors—the American public—in *every* area of life. And that is because it has rejected America's bedrock principle: "all men are created equal."

The Founders believed that elected representatives are responsible for "refining" and "enlarging" "the public view" through a constant give and take with those to whom they are responsible. They founded this country with the understanding that citizens are endowed with the right, the moral sense, and the responsibility to make just choices. The statesman's part is to discern and then persuade the American people to adopt the course most consistent with justice. If a statesman fails, either in discernment or per-suasion, he can be removed from office. There is nothing in the system that guarantees a perfect result—the people might not approve what is right, be persuaded to approve what is wrong, elect fools, or remove the wise from office. However, this system of mutual accountability respects the equal dignity of all and fosters the expectation that each will engage his highest reason, rather than his basest passions, in resolving the deep political questions that come before him.

Now consider how far this is removed from President Obama's governing principle, as exemplified in his statement to the *Times* reporter. The national "conversation" begins with the "experts." Obviously, this doesn't mean that every doctor, scientist, or ethicist will be consulted. Someone—perhaps the president himself—will decide who the *real* experts are. These hand-picked partisans will be account-able to no one but the one who appoints them. And one can imagine how the "conversation" will go. For starters, don't expect a lot of listening. As we've seen in debates on climate change, stem cell research, and the like, the experts don't persuade, but hector. If you disagree, you, by definition, are not an expert and therefore have no part in the "conversation." After a sufficient period of time to demonize any prominent voices that dissent, the "conversation" will be closed and it will be announced, in President Obama's terms, that the "time for talking is over." Of course, the experts will keep on talking—now as members of the board that determines whether your quality of life and the prospects for its improvement justify an addition to the national health care bill.

Alternatives to republican government, which is built upon the principle of human equality and the protection of God-given natural rights, have appeared in many forms down through the centuries. But in one sense, at least, they are all the same, dividing humanity into masters and slaves, lords and serfs, the ruling and the ruled.

## DEMOCRATS AND REPUBLICANS

Just more than a week before his death, Thomas Jefferson celebrated the growing consensus that "the mass of mankind has not been born with saddles on their backs, nor a favored few booted and spurred, ready to ride them." Thirty years later, Abraham Lincoln committed himself to the same underlying principle: "As I would not be a slave, so I would not be a master." All men are created equal—so no person is born with a right to compel the involuntary obedience of another. All men are created equal—so I should no more desire to exercise arbitrary power than to be subject to it.

Each spring, the Democratic and Republican faithful gather in various places around the country to celebrate the fathers of their respective parties, Jefferson and Lincoln. It is not clear that either of these men would be flattered by the perfunctory tributes, hack partisanship, and indigestible food for which these events are generally known. Fixing them, however, would require more than better speakers and better cooks. If either party's establishment were to investigate the party's ethical roots, it would find a common principle upon which Jefferson and Lincoln agreed and that both contemporary parties have, to varying degrees, abandoned: "all men are created equal." If this seems like an unlikely charge against today's Democrats and Republicans, it is only because we too often apply the principle only to issues like slavery, segregation, and similar questions of civil rights. Though even in this area, we could easily identify violations of the principle (like affirmative action, our fixation with identity politics, etc.), its implications are far broader, including the ways in which taxes are raised and spending is directed, the character of our middle class entitlements, and the Supreme Court's approach to judicial reasoning. If we are to appreciate how far we have abandoned the first moral principle of our regime, we must begin by understanding what Jefferson and Lincoln meant in declaring men to be equal and the implications of this principle for the relationships in a republic between citizens and their government and among citizens themselves.

## SUBJECTS AND CITIZENS

The difference between being a subject and being a citizen is more than a matter of semantics. It is more than the technical question of whether one resides in a monarchy or a republic. It is, at root, the difference between dependence and independence. A subject, willingly or not, understands that his prosperity—economic, social, and political—is the gift of men in authority over him, regardless of whether they have formal political office. He pays court to the great and looks upon his political leaders as potential benefactors, rather than stewards of his trust. It is to their whim that he must cater and to their will that he must conform. Indeed, in a nation where government controls access to essential services like health care, his life may very literally depend upon it. Thus, be his government authoritarian or popular, he is a subject: someone acting like less than a man before those presuming to be more than men.

While the citizen also submits to political authority, he does so in an entirely different way. He does not look to government for his daily bread or permission to pursue his calling, but for the even-handed protection of that which is already his. He recognizes that if government is essential to his prosperity and happiness, it does not thereby gain the right to take away his prosperity and happiness. For the citizen of a true republic, the law is not a tool of oppression or a mere imposition of power, but a rational principle binding upon his conscience even before it is binding upon his person. He is a man commanded first by reason and only then by the men who codify it.

Have we become a nation of subjects? Do we beg for a crumb (or a loaf) from the government's table—a tax break, regulatory loophole, special grant, or entitlement—that will make us or break us? President Obama's 2010 State of the Union Address certainly assumed we do: new benefits for those with student loans (with an extra bonus for those who add to the ever-expanding numbers in "public service"); special funds for high speed trains; rebates for making your home more energy efficient (to support "green jobs"); increased child care tax credits—and much, much more. And why should he think otherwise? How many town meetings did he hold on the campaign trail? And what is, by far, the most common question at a campaign town meeting? While a certain number will touch upon matters of principle or policy, one is struck by the rapidly-increasing proportion of questions that might be summarized: "If elected, what will you give me?" It is perhaps not surprising in our exhibitionist culture that no sense of shame prevents such questions from being asked, but one ought to be embarrassed for the republic that has nothing else to demand of its public "servants."

## LORDS AND CITIZENS

The most difficult test for a man is not whether he will submit to necessary oppression, but what he will do when it is finally thrown off. All men object to being slaves. But many do so only because they want to be masters. These have no objection to slavery in the principles of the institution, but only in the circumstantial fact of their position under it. Do you want to be free or do you want others to serve you?

Is a national election only about who will use the spoils of office—the power and the access to enjoy the fruits of others' labor? To the extent that this is so, we are not living in a republic, but in some sort of feudal system imposed upon our popular government, different only in the periodic rotation of lords and serfs or, in our case, Democrats and Republicans.

The spirit of the feudal lord is found in the political triumphalism that ends every policy debate with the mantra, "we won," and in every person who commands—and expects to be obeyed, looking upon those beneath him as the lab supplies for his social experiment. It is found in the presumption of policy-makers who speak and act as though the whole of the Gross Domestic Product is theirs to distribute. However pure their motives, however sound their judgments, however sincere their noblesse oblige, there is no escaping the fact that at the end of the day, the rest of us are meant to treat them as lords, whatever the official title before their name or the party letter after it.

There is an alternative to this, grounded in the principles of our republic. Just as there is a way for equal men to submit to political power, so too is there a way for equal men to exercise power, grounded in consent, rather than command. The republican statesman does not assume the self-evident goodness of his every intention or design, but labors to persuade, appealing to the common reason of his equals with seriousness and respect. Caricaturing the position of your opponents, heaping illimitable abuse upon your predecessors, and declaring rhetorical war against a long series of shadowy foes may please party hacks. But the true republican statesman knows that whatever authority he may exercise, his fellow citizens also have a right to pursue happiness and to be treated as those who are responsible for themselves rather than as cogs in another man's machine.

## REPUBLICAN EQUALITY

The idea of human equality is no charm with which to ward off the tendency of all governments to serve the interests of those with power and to demand fawning obedience from those without it. Popular government has never been an exception to this rule. In fact, the practical principle of democracy, "majority rules," can easily be perverted in this direction. When justly applied, the majority rules on behalf of the whole because those in the majority recognize the rest as their equals. But it is easy for the majority to follow a different principle—to rule on its own behalf as lords over subjects. The majority in a democracy naturally feels the weight of its quantitative superiority to those who oppose it. If all are equal individually, the majority is, in George Orwell's terms, *more* equal than the minority because of its greater numbers. And so, like Orwell's "two-legged" pigs, it struts about parading its pretense of power over man and against nature—the divine right of one hundred million kings.

When Alexis de Tocqueville described democracy in nineteenth century America, he warned against two apparently contradictory dangers. On the one hand, he observed, the majority could be an awful master, robbing its enemy not (only) of his goods, but of his independence of mind, social status, and self-respect. On the other hand, the same majority, he suspected, would be willing to submit to equality in slavery rather than allow anyone to exceed it in economic or social standing. And yet de Tocqueville saw then what we see now: The better angels of our nature might direct a well-disciplined and well-led people to reject prosperity by political command and social engineering in order to seek its good in the quiet life of private virtue and local association. Perhaps America would follow the sound principle laid down by George Washington for the foreign policy of our nation: No favors asked; none given. In doing so, she would neither pursue nor tolerate the use of public power for private gain.

## MIDDLE CLASS POLITICS

It would be difficult to find a more reliable political test in a republic than the simple question: Is a given policy or action suitable for masters and slaves or for a nation of equal citizens? Our contemporary politics shows the breadth of the applications of this rule.

Since 1992, the Democratic Party, or at least the part of it that wishes to win elections, has attempted to redefine itself as the champion of the middle class, rather than the poor. This has not been without its challenges. As Aristotle notes, those of moderate means are naturally a conservative element within a regime, restraining the extreme designs of rich and poor. Add to this the broad traditionalism of the American middle class—the prevailing commitments to family, honest labor, and the like—and one does not have a natural constituency for a "progressive" party bent on radical cultural transformation. There is, however, one quality (or weakness) of the middle class that creates opportunities for a government party: its desire for security.

Especially during times of economic difficulty, members of the middle class are painfully aware of the precariousness of their comfortable lives. When stock market losses and declining home values wipe out one-half of one's wealth in six months, it is natural to worry about the other half. When health care and education costs increase annually at double-digit rates, it is reasonable to wonder how long one can continue to consume either or both at the levels to which one has become accustomed. A promise of greater stability of life from government action, whether by regulatory decree or social welfare program, will attract many insecure middle class citizens, especially in such circumstances.

Of course, there are good economic reasons to doubt whether the government, by the mere force of its will and spending power, can actually maintain a certain standard of living over time, especially for the middle class—which is, itself, the principal generator of national wealth. But a glance at the means used to attempt this shows that trying to "insure" the middle class is even more ruinous politically than it is economically. For both Bill Clinton and Barack Obama, the key was a tax increase for the "rich" that was supposed to provide the necessary revenue for middle class benefits. This was justified with an arbitrary appeal to fairness—a poor mask for class envy.

In 1992, when Bill Clinton was first elected president, the top 5 percent of wage earners paid $218 billion in income tax while the bottom 75 percent paid $102 billion. After President Clinton's tax increase and President Bush's much larger tax cut, the ratio between the two numbers was far more dramatic: $615 billion for the top 5 percent and $141 billion for the bottom 75 percent (in 2006). The top 5 percent of wage earners paid 56 percent of the federal income tax the year before President Bush's "tax cuts for the rich"—and 60 percent six years later. Yet the rhetoric of the 2008 campaign was no different from that of 1992, with Senator Obama promising to raise taxes on the top 5 percent in order to provide social services and tax cuts to the rest. It is not at all clear that anything short of placing *all* of the tax burden upon the top 5 percent will satisfy contemporary notions of fairness—or perhaps the top 1 percent, that, in recent years, has paid more than the bottom 95 percent combined.

Setting aside the statistics, there is something fundamentally unrepublican in the naked appeal to middle class interest and the exploitation of middle class insecurity that has infected our politics—and not only on the Democratic side. There appears to be an assumption among the leaders and intellectuals of both parties that republican equality is at least politically—and probably morally—untenable. What remains then is only the contest over whose middle class program is most flattering, requires the least contemplation of the common good or the long-term interests of the country, and provides the most immediate, palpable, and generous benefits combined with the best disguised costs. Nothing illustrates this approach better than the efforts Democrats have made to mask the long-term consequences of their health care reforms. Combine ten years of taxes with six years of benefits and—voila!—you too can get Congressional Budget Office-certified deficit reduction. Whether one embraces this new American politics eagerly or reluctantly, the result is the same: a progressive acquiescence in the politics of masters and slaves and the progressive atrophying of our moral repugnance to it.

There are few appeals on the stump or comments around the water cooler more popular than a complaint against the insidious, amorphous "special interests" that get their way in Washington. President Obama declares that he is prepared to do battle with any of these who will stand in the way of his legislative program—and all are eager to applaud. But what if the *most* insidious special interest isn't the "fat-cat" bankers, Big Oil, or the United Auto Workers, but the American middle class? What if one looks behind the curtain of no-interest college loans, mortgage relief, ever-broadening health care entitlements and the rest— paid for by taxes on other people or by debt left to future generations—and finds nothing but the biggest, meanest, K street sharpie?

The remedy is simple, if difficult: a citizenry that rejects special benefits even when its immediate interest is involved and embraces the reality that the simple pursuit of republican equality is vastly more noble and honest—and the surer road to security too. We will know that Americans are really against "special interest" politics when politicians like Louisiana Senator Mary Landrieu and Nebraska's Ben Nelson *lose* their seats for having traded their approval of President Obama's health care overhaul for special favors for their states, when Congressmen of all stripes are too embarrassed to define their reelection campaign by their ability to deliver other people's money to their district or state, and when leaders of major corporations start thinking more about their customers than they do about the government regulators from whom they seek special privileges. Not before.

## OUR LORDS SUPREME

If it is difficult for Americans of moderate means to resist the temptation to use government power to circumvent the hard work that would otherwise be necessary to achieve economic security, our cultural elite has *entirely* embraced the temptation to enact its social agenda through judicial fiat. The lordly position assumed by the modern Supreme Court makes our elected leaders' arrogance look mild. Especially in cases that involve the great moral questions of our day, the Supreme Court has abandoned reasoned argument, the law's proper tool, and chosen instead to bully an unwilling people into proper submission.

Although it may not have been fully appreciated at the time it was announced, it is evident today that Roe v. Wade is the most important Supreme Court decision of the last fifty years. The majority opinion, written by Justice Blackmun, announced the overturning of all meaningful abortion laws on the books in 1973, uncovered a right to an abortion in the Fourteenth Amendment that no one had imagined existed for the first 105 years of its history, and cast aside hundreds of years of American and English legal tradition on the topic of abortion.

As striking as the immoderation of all this is, what is more striking still is the mode of Justice Blackmun's declaration. In its legal casebook form, the majority opinion runs approximately fifty-two pages. Of that whole, about one-fourth deals with the legal question of standing—the qualifications of the parties involved in the case. Another twenty pages comprises an historical survey of attitudes and laws on abortion from the ancient Greeks and Persians to the contemporary American Medical Association. As a result, it is not until the thirty-seventh page of the decision that Justice Blackmun turns his attention to the essential constitutional question: Is there, in fact, a right to an abortion?

Justice Blackmun's first paragraph amounts to a string of court precedents supposed to establish a constitutional right to privacy—not abortion—under any or all of the following amendments (or their "penumbras"): First, Fourth, Fifth, Ninth, and Fourteenth. The second paragraph begins by declaring that, wherever this right may actually be found, it "is broad enough to encompass a woman's decision whether or not to terminate her pregnancy" and proceeds to identify a number of significant hardships that would result from a woman's inability to secure a desired abortion. And that, with regard to the case for a constitutional right to an abortion, is that. There is nothing else. Justice Blackmun's "broad enough" has no more rational, legal, or moral justification than if he had simply said: "This is what I want." The rest of the decision involves Justice Blackmun's attempt to define the outer limits of this right, leading to his elaborately-constructed trimester system. It is literally the case, then, that there is not one sentence in the decision that attempts to make an argument for a constitutional right to abortion.

This is judicial pretense, not reason. That many people might desire it, that selected historical or contemporary groups approved of it—are these the foundations for *any* right? Every reasonable person must acknowledge that no right exists merely because of the breadth or depth of the human desire for it. And, of course, we can't seriously believe that Justice Blackmun cares whether the Persians exposed their infants or today's AMA endorses the *morality* of abortion. The countervailing beliefs of the followers of Hippocrates (summarized in the Hippocratic oath all doctors took practically until yesterday) and earlier statements of the AMA are as easily ignored as these approved. Seven justices shared a prejudice and made it law. Social liberals, when they could not persuade the American people of the merits of abortion on demand, joyfully embraced these black-robed sympathizers, who were willing to end the debate and make themselves the first American "death panel."

The implicit assertion of lordly prerogatives in *Roe* has become, in subsequent years, not so implicit. After the citizens of Colorado approved an amendment to their state constitution prohibiting the inclusion of homosexuals in the list of specially-protected classes in the state, the Supreme Court struck down the amendment as a violation of the equal protection clause of the (U.S. Constitution's) Fourteenth Amendment. While, once again, the Supreme Court majority's constitutional position was weak (using the principle of equality to invalidate an amendment prohibiting special privileges and protections?), the most striking aspect of the decision was its unconcealed contempt for the 53 percent of Colorado voters who approved the amendment. Nothing could have motivated the amendment, according to Justice Kennedy (writing for the majority), but "animus" against homosexuals. No principles of natural law, no concern for true equality or the rights of individual conscience, according to Kennedy, might have inspired support for this measure. Admittedly, this is a convenient assumption. After all, irrational hatred doesn't require a response. Assume that your opponents are unreasoning beasts and you can spare yourself the effort of answering them.

Here again, there is no attempt at rational persuasion, but rather an assertion of moral and intellectual superiority that forecloses all discussion. Since we are better (untainted by prejudice) and wiser—able to understand your motives (and the Constitution) better than you do—you must submit. Do not bother to respond. As your undoubted superiors, we need not answer your reasons or objections. Whatever the contemporary Supreme Court's self-understanding of its constitutional role may be, this is not the court for a republic.

In *Federalist* 78, Alexander Hamilton argued that the judiciary, if confined within its constitutional sphere, would be the branch of the government "least dangerous" to the rights of the people, since the court's power is confined to "judgment," rather than "force" (an executive power) or "will" (the legislature's prerogative). The essay goes on to make the case for the power of judicial review—the ability of the court to declare laws (or executive actions) unconstitutional. But Hamilton was quick to argue that this power is not the result of the court's superiority to the legislature, the executive branch, or the Constitution (and thereby the people). It is, rather, because the court, like the legislature and the executive branch, is *subject* to the Constitution (and thereby the people) that it must enforce the Constitution in preference to unconstitutional laws. What if, however, the court were to make the Constitution the instrument of its subjective will, rather than submitting to the words of the document in their proper linguistic and historical context?

By combining judicial and legislative powers, it would set itself up as master rather than servant and replace the sovereignty of the people with the sovereignty of the judiciary—with grave implications for our republic and our freedom. Hamilton concluded: "As liberty can have nothing to fear from the judiciary alone," it "would have every thing to fear from its union with either of the other departments."

## CONCLUSION

Since the 2008 election, much of our public discourse has centered on the question: In what new ways shall the federal government control our medical decisions? That question is not qualitatively different from most of the others that have dominated our public lives for the last two decades. Whether the subject is the cars we drive, the plumbing or the light bulbs in our homes, how we educate our children, or how we make a living, the one-size-fits-all approach of our ruling class is to order the detail of our lives more and more precisely. Regardless of the problem's nature, it has "solved" it by granting broad rulemaking power over us to boards, commissions, offices—to bureaucrats of every sort. As a result, we increasingly find ourselves subject to rulers not of our choosing and rules not of our making.

While the principle of human equality may be misapplied or abused, it is, nevertheless, the moral center of a republic. That "all men are created equal" means that there are no natural masters and slaves among men. To live consistently with this principle means neither seeking arbitrary power over others, nor submitting voluntarily to its exercise by others.

Alexander Hamilton opened the *Federalist Papers* by showing his readers what was—and remains—at stake in the American experiment with self-government: "It seems to have been reserved to the people of this country, by their conduct and example, to decide the important question, whether societies of men are really capable or not of establishing good government from reflection and choice, or whether they are forever destined to depend for their political constitutions on accident and force." The American Founders succeeded in showing that government based upon "reflection and choice" is possible. It has been the challenge and duty of each succeeding generation of Americans to demonstrate the possibility of *maintaining* such a government—of maintaining self-government—over time. Our generation can pass this test only by appreciating and living out the truth of human equality and demanding that our post-republican leaders do the same—or be replaced.

2

# Responsibility

*"the Laws of Nature and of Nature's God"*

—DECLARATION OF INDEPENDENCE, JULY 4, 1776

IN MARCH, 2009, President Obama issued a brief executive order calling upon the director of the National
Institutes of Health to develop new guidelines for federally-
funded research involving embryonic stem cells. As part of
this order, the president specifically rescinded restrictions
placed upon such research by President Bush that had aris-
en out of Bush's concern for the protection of early human
life. The NIH dutifully responded in July with guidelines
based on an entirely different set of concerns. The key step
to securing NIH approval for research on a new stem cell
line (derived from "unneeded" embryos produced by in
vitro fertilization—would-be "test tube babies") now would
be the "informed consent" of the donors. About one-third
of the document outlining the new guidelines is devoted
to making informed consent a practical reality. Donors are
protected from any influence judged to be improper—there
can be no promise of payment or benefits for donating and
no special appeals by would-be researchers. All relevant in-

formation about the research process and its consequences must be disclosed to the potential donors and they must be given the opportunity to rescind their consent until the research is actually performed. Nothing, in other words, can be permitted to get in the way of their perfectly free choice.

This new set of guidelines is eminently reasonable, even responsible, from one standpoint: Certainly, the idea of a couple creating human embryos to sell to the highest-bidding scientist is chillingly repulsive, as are high-pressure, utopian presentations by researchers to couples attempting to decide what to do with "their" embryos. These restrictions, however, do nothing about the real problem: Once the perfect conditions for "informed consent" are achieved, any couple, now regarded by law as the sovereign "creators" of these human beings in the earliest stages of development, is free to turn its progeny into the involuntary subject of a fatal experiment. What is there in this principle to keep two young scientists from creating their own embryos for purely experimental purposes? There is no consent, informed or otherwise, given by the microscopic party in this case—and no limit to the power imposed upon him or her. The real problem, then, is not in the *procedure* by which parents may dispose of their offspring, but in the *fact* that parents may dispose of their offspring—and ultimately in the fact that any human being has the arbitrary power of life and death over another.

As a result of this new policy, in December, 2009, the US government began to fund research on thirteen new lines of embryonic stem cells. This placed the government on one side of an ethical question that is at the heart of republican politics: Are human beings—whether one, a few, or many—able to do as they please with those who depend on them or are they bound by moral norms that exist beyond anyone's "consent?" Our republic was built upon the latter premise—and its survival depends upon our return to it.

## THE SECOND OF JULY

On July 2, 1776, the American colonies approved a resolution asserting that they "were and of right ought to be free and independent states." The goal of the war that had begun nearly fifteen months before at Lexington and Concord was now clear: compel Britain to acknowledge the political independence of the United States. Such a statement of policy was all that was needed to secure the aid of France. But the Continental Congress, as we all know, did not conclude its work on July 2. For two days, the members carefully revised and deliberated upon a document that would "declare the reasons that impel them to the separation"—the Declaration of Independence. Why did they bother? Because, as reasonable, morally responsible human beings, they knew they had to.

The American Founders understood that right reason, not force, is the final argument in politics. Of course, political practice often tells a different story, but "a decent respect to the opinions of mankind requires" that good reasons be given for political actions. We do not ask animals to justify their actions. But, because human beings, unlike animals, are rational creatures, capable of giving reasons and judging the reasons for actions given by others, we expect even a young child to justify his behavior. To make a revolution requires more than guns; it requires a cause capable of securing the approval of a "candid world."

The Founders did not seek the approval of men, however, as if they were their own ultimate lawgivers. Instead, they sought the recognition by others that their actions measured up to the standard against which all human actions are judged: the "Laws of Nature and of Nature's God." Because such a law exists, human beings have no right to define what is good or just merely according to their own individual or collective judgment. Indeed, we must all, like the Founders, submit our actions, words, and even "intentions" to the approval of the "Supreme Judge of the world."

Recognition of our moral responsibility is essential for the citizens of a republic. A man who believes that his own will is the final arbiter on all moral questions will see no reason for the moral restraint republics are built upon. While he may be quick to assert his rights, the corresponding responsibility to recognize the rights of others will seem arbitrarily imposed and only an impediment to his pleasure. Liberated from moral norms, he will be a beast, not a free man.

Perhaps this language seems too strong. Today's Americans, after all, seem to maintain a reasonable measure of civilized behavior despite their general skepticism concerning moral absolutes. Nevertheless, the political consequences of rejecting the fact of moral responsibility are evident all over the political spectrum—from education policy (in the apotheosis of self-esteem) to beggar-thy-neighbor tax laws and health care legislation. More than anywhere else, however, it is in debating and (increasingly) in legislating on issues involving life and death, including the legality of abortion, embryonic stem-cell research, and cloning that we see a plain truth: Human beings unwilling to submit to an authority beyond their own judgment have only force, enslaved by personal interest, to guide them.

## AUTONOMY

As the debate over slavery in the United States intensified, Stephen Douglas, senator from Illinois, believed that he had a thoroughly American way of settling it: popular vote. Why not, asked Douglas, allow the people of each state or territory to decide if they want slavery? After all, he reasoned, each community made its own decisions about whether to allow liquor, what to do about public schools, and a thousand other questions. Why should the issue of slavery be any different? Anticipating the most obvious response, he revealed an understanding of politics far removed from that of the Founders: "It is no answer to this argument to say that slavery is an evil, and hence should not be tolerated. You must allow the people to decide for themselves whether it is a good or an evil." Douglas might have defended "local control" of slavery on other grounds. He could have argued that though slavery is evil, it might still be tolerated (at least temporarily) to avoid an even greater evil (social disruption or interracial warfare). He could then have suggested that it was reasonable for local voters to decide whether this toleration was necessary for a given state or territory in a particular circumstance.

Instead, however, Douglas asserted that the people have the right and power to determine the *morality* of slavery: whether it is good or evil. That is because, for Douglas, there was nothing intrinsically right or wrong about slavery—or really anything else. Autonomous people, acting on their own authority, would settle the question—at least for a day (or until Douglas was in the White House). What is to guide the voters' judgment? Without a universal standard of right and wrong, there is little left but the individual interest of each voter. For those with the prospect of being masters (or the popular leaders of those masters), there is a powerful temptation to approve what is to their selfish advantage— and no moral principle to oppose it. Human responsibility thus reinforces human equality, while autonomy naturally divides men on the basis of interest or power.

In light of the fact that slavery was abolished less than a decade after Douglas's remark, to no one's regret today, this episode might have been an historical footnote except for one fact: Douglas's attempt to (re-)define the heart of American government has been endorsed by the contemporary Supreme Court.

In Planned Parenthood v. Casey (1992), the court majority defended the right to an abortion with an understanding of liberty completely divorced from any moral foundations: "At the heart of liberty is the right to define one's own concept of existence, of meaning, of the universe, and of the mystery of human life. Beliefs about these matters could not define the attributes of personhood were they formed under compulsion of the State."

Liberty, according to the Supreme Court, is fundamentally concerned with the right to define reality for oneself. There is nothing that is given, no fixed point of truth. Hence, it would be wrong for the state to take any position on the "mystery of human life" (with obvious implications for abortion policy) since that would prevent individuals from *defining* "the attributes of personhood." My human dignity (and yours), according to the court, exists only in so far as someone else is willing to recognize it.

Despite obvious differences in context, the principles of Douglas and *Casey* are the same: The human will is the highest moral force in the universe. This idea, one must admit, has a certain attraction. Its consequences, however, do not: human beings with the god-like right and power to decide who is a man and who is a beast. The self-interestedness and fickleness of human judgment should make us wary of granting such power to anyone, including ourselves. If men are free to define the order of the universe, it can only be because there is nothing in any of us that cries out for recognition and respect—no irreducible minimum regard demanded by the objective fact of our existence. We should not be surprised then that claims of human autonomy arose in the debates over two of the most fundamental denials of human dignity—slavery and abortion—and continue to be applied to the most pressing moral questions of our day. What is a man after you have taken away his right to the product of his labor? An appendage of your body, an extra set of arms and legs to work while you eat. What is a man whose very existence is subject to your arbitrary will? An object, a thing, mere refuse waiting to be discarded.

One may be slightly troubled by such observations without being fundamentally shaken so long as one has no practical expectation of being the slave or the unborn child. But if force becomes the only argument in politics, one may not always find oneself in such an enviable position. As Lincoln warned the slaveowner: "And if he [the slave] can make it his interest, he has the right to enslave you." A government agency tasked with reducing the national health care bill may decide that your treatment is too expensive or too unlikely to succeed. A panel of experts may decide that once your quality of life falls below a certain threshold, your life is subhuman and ultimately disposable. And even if we never suffer the logical consequences of our principles, are we really sure that our highest purpose is the unrestrained pursuit of interest and pleasure, regardless of the harm to others?

## RESPONSIBILITY

Thomas Jefferson had a different view of the role of the people in a free government. In his First Inaugural Address, he placed an important qualification on the limits of majority rule: "Though the will of the majority is in all cases to prevail, that will to be rightful must be reasonable; that the minority possess their equal rights, which equal law must protect, and to violate would be oppression." It is not necessary to give up on popular government in order to recognize the natural limits to the power of the majority. Can it be reasonable to use one's vote to deny the very principle that justifies that vote? And yet a vote that undermines the equal rights of the minority does just that. If resolving political differences by voting is a reasonable implication of human equality, using votes to deny that equality is not only immoral but irrational. Of course, it is practically possible for people to do all sorts of irrational things, but there is something essentially human that is compromised in such cases. To be "reasonable"—to be "rightful"—demands the recognition of the intrinsic qualities of personhood possessed by one's fellow men. Rather than denying the existence of such qualities with the modern Supreme Court, at least one justice in Lincoln's day believed that they were the beginning of political reasoning.

Justice McLean, writing in dissent in the notorious *Dred Scott* case, would not—could not—look at Dred Scott as a simple article of property: "A slave is not a mere chattel. He bears the impress of his Maker, and is amenable to the laws of God and man; and he is destined to an endless existence." Man is not the master of *this* universe. He is the creature, not the Creator. He is the judged, not the Judge. And yet, almost paradoxically, the recognition of his subjection to the divine, rather than undermining his moral significance, is consistent with and even the basis for his true dignity. To be morally responsible is to be elevated above the common creature—to be distinct from the amoral beast.

Moral responsibility, then, is one of man's highest privileges. We should no more thank the Supreme Court of *Dred Scott* and *Casey* for liberating us from it than we would thank the transnational elites who are eager to impose upon us arbitrary obligations to the environment or the Third World. To be subject to the just and reasonable commands of the wise God of the universe is right and ennobling; to be subject to the subjective will of spiteful masters is quite the opposite.

## SCIENCE UNBOUND

If the Declaration of Independence is correct, then all political actions must be judged against what is right. In a republic, then, it is not enough to inquire into what the majority *can* do; one must ask what the majority *may* do. Everyone knows that five boys can take a sixth boy's milk money—and everyone knows that they shouldn't, even if they can get away with it. The majority's actions, even when physically or legally unrestrained, must demonstrate its submission to the given moral order binding all men. Personal or collective interest may not trump the intrinsic rights and dignity of others. It is with these limitations in mind that we must consider the great threats to human dignity posed in our own time by the ethical liberation of science for the unrestrained pursuit of medical advance.

Aristotle called political science the "master art" because it determined the limits of the practice of all the other arts. Today, we would rightly object to a government that took upon itself the responsibility of settling important theological questions or decreeing the next advance in computer operating systems. Could anyone reasonably object, however, to a government that prohibited human sacrifice or prevented an operating system from disseminating a virus that did irreparable harm to other computers? If not, then why is it so common to hear that science ought to be freed from the restraint of government? Why is it considered anti-science to suggest that medical research respect the same bounds the American Founders applied to their politics—the limits of human dignity and respect? President Obama asserted in his Inaugural Address that he would "restore science to its rightful place"—but is that as master or servant of men? It is important not to pose a false choice between an unlimited science and a science subordinated to arbitrary political agendas. Instead, responsible limits must be placed and maintained on biomedical research and engineering to ensure the submission of science to objective moral principles.

The common quality in almost every act of political injustice is the conflict between interest and right—the powerful temptation to act for one's own (individual or group) benefit regardless of the price to others. This temptation is magnified when the prospective benefit is especially great and desirable, when the "others" are weak, comparatively few, and voiceless, and, more generally, whenever there is a great (real or apparent) disproportion between the value of the interest secured and the value of the right violated. Each of these factors is at work in the debate over activities like (embryonic) stem cell research and human cloning.

There seems to be little that contemporary Americans won't do to extend their lives or improve their health. The possibility of discovering therapeutic treatments for devastating conditions like paralysis or Parkinson's disease or finding ways to slow the aging process creates a powerful incentive to extend the boundaries of scientific research—and there is no adult who can safely say that he will never have a use for such treatments. Meanwhile, the human embryos that might be created or destroyed in such research are supposed to be comparatively few and are certainly silent. As powerfully influenced as we are by our sensory perceptions and personal affections, it takes a substantial act of will and moral imagination even to recognize the humanity that the embryo shares with the spinal injury victim or the aging grandmother. It is much easier to exercise our constitutional "right" and define these embryos, if not out of existence, then at least out of the human species. But who is *really* ready to take the lives of as comparatively few as one hundred innocent people even to benefit 300 million? How much "better" if the Supreme Court has relieved us of this moral dilemma? Put all this together and how surprised should we be to find that the temptation to create and destroy microscopic (human?) life—not for sadistic pleasure but to alleviate enormous human suffering—is so great?

An argument sufficient to meet this challenge must be grounded in the indefeasible value of human life and the moral seriousness of responsible men. Human beings free to define the "attributes of personhood" in a case so unlikely to yield an impartial judgment are almost certain to choose their interest over an apparently abstract right. But this, of course, is no occasion for concern on the part of those who have already judged the embryo to be of insignificant value—to be *not* innocent when proven useful. Nevertheless, in doing so they act upon principles contrary to their true interest and ultimately incompatible with the security of the life they are laboring to extend or improve. There is no reason, within the logic of the right to define what it means to be a person, why the line must be drawn in the womb or the laboratory. That there may be few inclined at present to define away the humanity of some number of adults or children does not mean that this must always be the case— and there is no security against this happening within the world of human autonomy. We have too much evidence too recently compiled of what happens when European Jews, the bourgeois class or others becomes respectably despised, then legally abused, and finally murderously destroyed. And there are always a few, like Dostoevsky's Grand Inquisitor or our contemporary Supreme Court, ready to supply the argument to justify it and free us from the burden of our own moral responsibility.

## CONCLUSION

Not all slopes are equally slippery. The logic of each principle upon which human beings act does not necessarily unfold with perfect precision over the course of time. This is true in part because individual men are able to live almost indefinitely with unreconciled contradictions between their principles and their practice. This is also true because there are moments in an individual's or a nation's life when the multiplying effects of bad habits and ideas become so evident that they are abandoned. But is it wise simply to hope that we will never suffer the worst consequences of our bad ideas—the loss of our dignity or even our lives? Should we ignore the fact that even the drunk who sobers up has often already done great harm to himself and others?

Ultimately, the citizens of a republic must be willing to acknowledge that the foundation for their dignity and the security for their rights is their moral responsibility to their Creator. Because ours is the privilege of self-government, we must choose. But because we are morally responsible, we must choose well. To deny this is to repeat the sin of Adam and cast ourselves out of the fruitful garden onto the unyielding ground of power, force, and interest. There one may find despots and slaves, but no free men.

# 3

# Honor

*"preserve, protect, and defend the Constitution"*

—U.S. CONSTITUTION, SEPTEMBER 17, 1787

As PART of her 2009 "White House Christmas Special," Oprah Winfrey asked President Obama what grade he thought he deserved for the first year of his presidency. The president answered that he thought that he had earned a "good, solid B+" and that his grade would rise to an A- if health care reform passed before the end of the year (not quite). He went on to explain the reasoning behind his grade, citing a variety of domestic and foreign policy accomplishments despite having, as he claimed, "inherited the biggest set of challenges of any president since Franklin Delano Roosevelt."

There were three problems with the President's list. First, he claimed credit for whatever benefits the actions of the Treasury and Federal Reserve achieved with policies adopted four months before his presidency began and for a recovery that started before almost any of the dollars in his trademark "stimulus" package had been spent. Then there were the pseudo-achievements that any teacher will recognize from the pleas of students for a better grade: I tried hard; I came to class; I participated a lot. For President Obama, these included things like "resetting" America's image around the world. Lastly, and most importantly, the president praised his efforts "to pass the most significant piece of social legislation since social security." The word "significant" tells the whole story. When presidents keep score according to the size and scope of their new entitlements, we are very far from the Founders' government. There is, in fact, really only one standard by which any American president ought to be judged: the degree to which he has lived up to his oath to "preserve, protect, and defend the Constitution of the United States."

There is nothing inherently wrong with anyone wanting a string of A's on the report card of history. The Founders themselves had a keen sense of their own individual desires for honor. But nearly all recognized that their honor depended upon the success of their noble work—establishing an American republic that was both stable and good—and that the honor of their successors would depend upon their ability, in the words of Abraham Lincoln, to "perpetuate our institutions." This did not mean that every part of the constitutional structure had to remain as established in 1789. The Constitution itself includes the means of its own amendment. But whatever changes would come over time were not to be the result of decisions made by office-holders on their own authority. After all, the very positions they fill are the creation of the document to which they swear to submit. These oaths are serious because the Constitution is serious—the basic contract by which we live as a people and define the work that officeholders will do on our behalf. Thus, in the United States, we need statesmen, not demagogues, office-seekers, or Caesars. And it is the job of the American people to demand them.

## A STATESMAN, NOT A DEMAGOGUE

The short-term judgment of any presidency is almost universally acknowledged to be the president's current "approval rating," which is breathlessly announced, with whatever insignificant change that has taken place, in the newspapers and cable news crawlers each day. This is probably why the most common Republican response to President Obama's "B+" was to bring up the fact that he had the lowest approval rating ever for a first-year president. But the public's approval rating is as meaningless as the president's self-evaluation if it is not a measure of President Obama's fidelity to the Constitution.

The president's poll standing *was* in many ways shocking, however, given the enthusiasm that surrounded his presidential campaign and the over-the-top flattery that reverberated between his supporters and himself. "We are the ones we've been waiting for" he told the crowd on Super Tuesday. When he clinched the Democratic nomination, he took it to the next level: "If we are willing to work for it, and fight for it, and believe in it, then I am absolutely certain that, generations from now, we will be able to look back and tell our children that this was the moment when we began to provide care for the sick and good jobs to the jobless; this was the moment when the rise of the oceans began to slow and our planet began to heal; this was the moment when we ended a war, and secured our nation, and restored our image as the last, best hope on Earth." On

June 3, 2008, a date which was to live in "famy," the crowd screamed in approval as the people of the United States and their Democratic party nominee assumed powers no mere man had ever possessed—the ability to control the oceans and to "heal" the planet.

The fatuous call and response between a candidate and his supporters on election night is not, however, the most perverse form of demagoguery to plague a popular government. Much worse is the cheap populism that trades on the lowest impulses of the crowd and the easiest political stereotypes. Blame the insurance companies, the bankers, the oil executives and the like for every social problem and you've done two things: first, let 98 percent of the American public off the political hook and second, created a dragon so big and so bad that only the strong arm of the federal government can slay it.

President Obama responded to Scott Brown's incredible special election victory in Massachusetts by getting out in front of the parade. Brown's win was, according to the President, really just the aftershock of his own. To prove the point, President Obama spent the rest of the week burnishing his populist bona fides by picking a fight with the banks and seeing how much wealth he could drive out of the stock market. As at other times, the President cozied up to the American people by condescendingly assuring them that their envy was virtuous even as he fundamentally diminished them in presupposing their helplessness against their enemies. This is diametrically opposed to the principles of republican statesmanship.

A right understanding of the citizenry of a republic neither allows the people the privilege of abandoning their moral responsibilities nor pretends that they are helpless children in need of the paternal care of a "public servant." True statesmen treat the voting public as reasonable adults who, while given to selfish desires and self-justifying rationalizations, recognize the high calling of the title "citizen." Long before the French Revolutionaries turned it into a badge of radical egalitarianism, the name "citizen" was bestowed upon those who enjoyed the dignity, in Aristotle's terms, of governing and being governed in turn. A truly republican statesman is a leader of citizens and a citizen himself who is prepared to lend his labor and wisdom to the community for a time to clarify the choices before the public and to persuade them to choose what is good. He is neither the indispensable guardian of the flock nor the prostrated suppliant of "King Numbers," but the earnest counselor and just leader of his equals. He does not seek the adulation of the crowd, but the respect of his countrymen and the verdict of history that he contributed to the preservation of the republic.

## A STATESMAN, NOT AN OFFICE-SEEKER

When distinguished political scientist David Mayhew attempted to determine how much of the individual and collective behavior of modern Congressmen he could explain by assuming that their first (and, in some cases, only) priority was re-election, his conclusion was: pretty much all of it. Nevertheless, one Amazon.com reviewer gave Professor Mayhew's book only one star since, he argued, it shouldn't take 192 pages to figure out that members of Congress want to be re-elected. While this may be true, what Professor

Mayhew argued was several degrees more subtle: That members of Congress rarely, if ever, act contrary to their electoral interest, whatever ideological or public-spirited explanation they may give for their actions. Again, the cynic asks: Where's the news? If there still is none, this would only demonstrate the dwarfish stature of our present ruling class rather than a necessary condition of our popular government.

As everyone who has taken a basic class in American government knows, our system of checks and balances was designed to keep each branch of the federal government within its bounds. It would work, in the words of James Madison (in *Federalist* 51), by "giving to those who administer each department the necessary constitutional means and personal motives to resist encroachments of the others . . . . Ambition must be made to counteract ambition." The maintenance of limited, constitutional government did not depend, according to Madison, on each officeholder voluntarily surrendering his ambition for power. So long as the members of each branch defended their own prerogatives with the powers they had been granted in the Constitution, it would be impossible for the members of the other two branches to extend their authority beyond its constitutional bounds. Ambition, then, would counteract ambition.

Not all sorts of ambition are the same, however. The Constitution was designed to channel the ambition that seeks greatness and to counter that which leads to mere corruption. Considerably different and more dangerous is the base ambition of the mere office-seeker who, to keep his job or seat "safe," may find it convenient to allow other branches or agencies to draw his legitimate power into their sphere. What better suits the needs of Congressmen consumed with reelection than allowing the courts, for example, to make all the hard decisions on controversial social issues like abortion, gay marriage, capital punishment, and affirmative action? When necessary, they can complain loudly about "judicial activism," while quietly being spared the sorts of votes that require uncomfortable explanations to one's constituency.

The second section of Article III of the Constitution allows Congress to remove whole categories of cases from the (appellate) jurisdiction of the federal courts. A Congress properly jealous of its power to legislate in these important areas of social policy might easily use this provision to rein in the courts, but our legislators do not. This tells us more about the true ambitions of Congressmen than any of their complaints about an overactive judiciary.

The same story can be told in the extensive delegation of law-making powers to commissions and bureaucratic agencies. Why is it that the EPA, rather than Congress, has declared carbon dioxide a dangerous pollutant (please try to breathe out less often)? Why are the most important decisions in key areas of policy made by "independent agencies" like the Federal Reserve? Why not let the bureaucrats and regulators with real job security make the tough calls, while reserving the right to join the populist outcry against them if they can't be buried in a late Friday afternoon press release?

Equally advantageous to legislative office-seekers are the commissions that members of Congress have established in recent years to limit their political liability for unpopular decisions. One of the first was the base-closing commission established after the Cold War to put together an annual list of unnecessary military bases that would be presented to Congress for a simple up or down vote—providing at least some measure of cover for those who were unable to "protect" a base in their home state or district. Similar commissions have been established to make difficult decisions about topics as varied as post office locations and criminal sentencing guidelines—and now deficit reduction—populated by those far removed from any real accountability to the people.

By this point, it must begin to be clear why a government overrun with office-seekers is a danger to our republic. The two fundamental checks on government power—the two basic ways in which our regime is preserved in its constitutional purity—are both undermined when re-election is the chief end of our leaders. First, the internal system of checks and balances atrophies as powers intended to combat extra-constitutional actions go unused. This is not just a problem of the legislative branch. One of the early tests of President Bush's domestic leadership came in March, 2002, when he was presented with the McCain-Feingold campaign finance reform bill. Although he had "reservations about the constitutionality" of parts of the bill, he signed it anyway, in the apparent (though unfulfilled—until January, 2010) expectation that the Supreme Court would strike down the objectionable provisions and spare him a politically unpopular veto. It would, in fact, be a record five and a half years into his presidency before President Bush vetoed his first bill, neglecting until well into his second term a power that was granted especially to enforce the limits of the Constitution.

The second problem with a ruling class of office-seekers is that in so far as they are able to isolate themselves from electoral accountability, they undermine the ability of the people to change policy by changing officeholders. When members of Congress or the president delegate key decisions to those over whom the people have no control, it becomes more and more difficult to imagine how the voters can play their intended part in curtailing government overreach. What does it matter if a few D's are replaced with a few R's, if most of the people stretching government power to its furthest limits are members of the federal employees union, judges with life-time appointments, or heads of agencies unaccountable to the public? And this does not even account for the additional diminishing of electoral accountability that results from the fact that 62 percent of federal spending (even before the new health care program goes into full effect) covers mandatory expenditures for entitlement programs and interest on the national debt. With so much of the national budget on auto-pilot, political leaders can easily escape responsibility for the extraordinary spending and deficit figures that have, in recent years, become quite ordinary.

Despite the obvious flaws in their character, the root of the problem of office-seeking politicians is in the system of profligate spending and influence-peddling that attracts them and in the public that (re-)elects them. In any society at any time there are plenty of people eager to be an "insider" in a participatory kleptocracy, with all the opportunities to reward friends (beginning with "number one") and punish enemies that this creates. The biggest challenge for these would-be political drones is to come up with the cause that will make their campaign about more than getting the other guy out so that they can get in. There is no need to do great things when all the social and material comforts of life are available to those who simply manage to stay in office long enough to retire to the lucrative consulting and lobbying contracts that any well-connected former Congressman is able to attract. There is also no need to do great things when the local public is satisfied so long as it gets its share (or maybe a bit more) of the public works projects, research dollars, defense contracts, and the rest of the presents within the government's gift. Reform too often begins in someone else's home.

It is easy to scoff at Alaska's "bridge to nowhere" or lampoon the late John Murtha's $100 million defense appropriation for John Murtha Johnstown-Cambria County Airport (with fewer than thirty passengers per day). Of course, Murtha was elected eighteen times by the people of Pennsylvania's twelfth congressional district, so the locals didn't appear to mind - and they aren't any worse than the rest of us. The reason Congressmen fear voting to close a military base in their home district, whatever its real usefulness, is that they fear their vote will be a strong weapon against them in their next political campaign. And the reason they fear this is that it is true. The easiest and most nonpartisan political points an election opponent can score come from standing with the locals against the "Washington politician" who has "lost touch" with his constituency – who hasn't been able to deliver like Murtha did. Every hack political consultant knows how to write that press release. So long as it works, office-seekers will dominate Congress. And so long as office-seekers dominate Congress, the power of the federal government will grow and the ability of the American public to stop that growth will shrink—and more office-seekers will run for Congress.

## A STATESMAN, NOT A CAESAR

Early in his public career, Abraham Lincoln warned the Young Men's Lyceum about the sort of politician who would not be satisfied with merely preserving the Founders' republic—an American Caesar. Those of the "tribe of the eagle" or the "family of the lion," said Lincoln, would seek to make their mark by tearing down the republic they had inherited and building a new regime for their own glory.

In the more than one and a half centuries since Lincoln issued his warning, the United States has been graciously spared the worst sort of Caesar—one who would literally overthrow the regime in both form and substance in the manner of Julius Caesar himself. Lesser sorts of Caesars, however, bent on recasting our regime in their own favorite mold, have not been lacking. The threat today is two-fold. The most obvious is the ongoing attempt by the progressive wing of the Democratic Party, led by President Obama, to remake America in the model of a European-style social democracy. The centerpiece of this effort is, of course, the creation of a massive new entitlement through "comprehensive health care reform."

There is now three generations worth of evidence, going back to the era of the New Deal, that significant expansions of the welfare state are very difficult to undo. There are several reasons why this is the case. Most obviously, one of the two major parties in the nation is permanently and ideologically committed to the defense of such programs and can be counted on to use every political tactic available to protect them. Second, once a program is established, it creates a large number of beneficiaries who are likely to defend the program regardless of its cost or their other political commitments. As a result, a significant number of citizens who are otherwise opposed to "big government" nevertheless join in the opposition to any changes to programs from which they receive substantial benefits. Third, and perhaps most important, once a federal program exists, the state, local, and private means by which the given service was previously provided wither away or disappear altogether. As a result, it becomes increasingly difficult for most people even to imagine a world without it. It is this last factor that is most significant in the current attempt to establish a government-directed health care system. When fully-operational, such a system will change the structure of American society quickly and decisively, so that alternatives that involve less government rather than more will, for all practical purposes, disappear. For all of these reasons, unflagging efforts are necessary to repeal the health care bill before it becomes fully operational in 2014.

No less transformational could be the consequences of current attempts to create a whole new model of public-private economic "partnership" built upon an almost entirely government-created "green" economy. Establishing a government-mandated price for carbon, whether through the proposed cap-and-trade bill, EPA fiat, or some other means, would change the financial structure of the entire energy industry by making fossil fuels (oil, coal, natural gas)—currently supplying 90 percent of the energy used in the United States—artificially expensive. Combined with various government subsidies already in place, including $80 billion of government "investment" in green projects in the stimulus bill alone, this policy would increase the market share of alternative energy products without requiring their producers to do anything to make them better—cheaper, more efficient, etc. The alternative energy industry would, as a result, make lots of money simply because the government conferred artificial value on otherwise unmarketable products. Every company in this industry would know that its profitability was dependent upon the maintenance of this competitive advantage and, in general, good relations with political leaders and regulators. Thus, the key players in the new market for energy would not just be different in name, but different in kind: government clients, rather than free market winners. If we add to this the expanded government involvement in the financial sector justified by the fall of 2008 meltdown, but further institutionalized each day, and the health care takeover already discussed, it is evident that a very large portion of the American economy is being moved from the private sphere of individual choice to the public sphere of government compulsion. In this new America, the votes will still be counted every other year, but the fundamental character of our regime will have been altered dramatically and perhaps permanently.

How can all this be forced into our existing constitutional framework? The short answer is that it cannot. Then why won't the Supreme Court, at least, stop it? Because, for at least seventy years, the Supreme Court has been unwilling to enforce the constitutional limits on federal power in all areas that have any plausible relation to the national

economy. Here, once again, ambition has failed to counteract ambition. It is not surprising (though still in most cases
blameworthy) that Congress and the president have, partic-
ularly in response to crises (real or supposed), attempted to
expand the scope of their authority. If the Supreme Court,
even with only the lesser motive of protecting its relative
position within our tripartite system, were to enforce the
clear constitutional limits of federal authority, such efforts
by the other two branches would fail. But, for the most part,
the Supreme Court, rather than countering the expansive
tendencies of the legislative and executive branches, has,
instead, reinforced them, creating a three-headed Caesar
laboring for the indefinite expansion of federal power.

Thomas Jefferson and James Madison worried very
early in our history that it would not be safe to rely upon
the Supreme Court to enforce the limits of the Constitution
since the Court, as part of the federal government, could
not be trusted to be an even-handed arbiter in disputes
over the division of state and federal power. The most serious dangers of this problem were slow to germinate. In the
last century, however, we have seen very clearly the fruit
of combining an ever-growing deference to the Supreme
Court in resolving constitutional questions with the Court's
embrace of the centralized administrative state. The alternative, however, is not the neutered judiciary that Jefferson,
at least, often advocated. For nearly thirty-five years, Chief
Justice John Marshall, a contemporary of both Jefferson
and Madison, labored to establish a federal judiciary with
its full constitutional vigor and to protect legitimate federal
authority from the then-powerful reach of ambitious states.
This was no more and no less than his responsibility (and

that of his peers), whatever the abuses later court sophists have illegitimately heaped upon his solid foundation.

While the day may come when an American Caesar does away with our republic for good, the thousand cuts of our mini-Caesars have already drawn more blood than it is safe to lose. Ask yourself this: How many people have a (short-term) economic stake in small(er) government today? Nearly half of American households pay no net income tax at all. Add to this number those who are government employees, work for companies or non-profits that are dependent upon government contracts, and work in industries heavily subsidized by government grants. Then include anyone not already counted who depends upon benefits received from an entitlement program, a government-guaranteed loan, etc., etc. How many independent citizens are left? The greatest impediment to restoring something of the Founders' vision is not the impersonal "modern conditions" that supposedly make our political behemoth necessary or inevitable, but the fact that too many people eat what they suppose is Caesar's bread and cheer his circuses.

## CONCLUSION

Can the American people really elect true statesmen to replace the current stale mix vastly overpopulated by demagogues, office-seekers, and pint-sized Caesars? This would require of us levels of discernment and political virtue not seen in some years. But there have been times in our history when demagogues have been exposed, office-seeker scorned, and Caesars unapplauded. There have been individual leaders who held themselves and their colleagues to a higher standard and realized, at least in part, the republican ideal in their honorable service to our nation. Moreover, though the Founders had plenty of skepticism concerning the motives and measures of men, they believed that the American people could maintain a healthy republic. James Madison said as much in *Federalist* 55: "As there is a degree of depravity in mankind which requires a certain degree of circumspection and distrust, so there are other qualities in human nature which justify a certain portion of esteem and confidence.   Republican government presupposes these qualities in a higher degree than any other form. Were the pictures which have been drawn by the political jealousy of some among us faithful likenesses of the human character, the inference would be that there is not sufficient virtue among men for self-government; and that nothing less than the chains of despotism can restrain them from destroying and devouring one another."

Before we fit ourselves for the chains offered by our present ruling class and reverse the choice of our forefathers to be Americans, rather than Europeans, let us recall the picture of statesmanship drawn by the Founders and insist that those who take oaths of office take them seriously and work hard faithfully to maintain our republican way of life from one generation to the next.

# 4

## Justice

*"an improper or wicked project"*

—James Madison,
*Federalist* 10, November 22, 1787

H  UMAN EQUALITY requires that law treat all citizens in
the same way. Nevertheless, it is the experience of almost all people under almost all governments that the law
benefits the well-connected at the expense of the rest. In
popular governments like ours, policy-makers negotiate with
"stakeholders" for the sake of mutual advantage, trading subsidies, tax breaks, and regulatory favors for political support.
The results are thoroughly unrepublican—and thoroughly
unjust—the sorts of policies and programs the Founders did
not hesitate to call "improper or wicked." In recent years, we
have become too accustomed to such politics, but the perva-
siveness and brazenness of the Obama Administration's use
of these tactics to move its health care agenda forward has
seemingly reawakened our repugnance to them.

In relatively plain view, President Obama cut deals
with the various groups he feared might oppose his health
care bill, guaranteeing their profits at the expense of their

independence. Pharmaceutical companies were prom-
ised a cap on the profits the government would confiscate
and administration opposition to importing drugs from
abroad. The AARP, with its own stake in the health insurance business, was persuaded to hold its tongue despite a
half a trillion dollars in cuts to the Medicare program dear
to its members. The American Medical Association's opposition to a government-sponsored insurance program in
June, 2009, was turned into an endorsement of a House bill
creating one in just five weeks with a promise to eliminate a
cut in Medicare payments to doctors.

Those who wouldn't take the carrot, got the stick. At a
New Hampshire town hall meeting, for example, President
Obama suggested that doctors prefer to amputate the feet
of diabetics rather than manage the disease in order to get
the $30-50,000 reimbursement (actually $500-$700) that an
amputation brings. In his health care speech before a joint
session of Congress, he claimed (incorrectly) that a man
from Illinois had died because he lost his health insurance
in the middle of a chemotherapy cycle for failing to report a
minor case of gallstones. Thus, even while President Obama
bought the silence of the health care industry, he simultane-
ously demonized it, attempting to convince the American
people that he was their champion and protector.

In the Obama-era, policy is now made by presiden-
tially-appointed czars in cooperation with business and
non-profit stakeholders. Who counts in this system? Not
the voting and tax-paying public, whose "stake" in what
happens to their lives and property is ignored. This became all the more evident as public support for health care
reform collapsed during the months-long congressional

debate over the House and Senate bills. Instead, the true players are those with the right political connections and lobbyists. Once they are "on board," the ship is ready to sail. And once the ship sails, it is the same faction of the well-connected and approved that mans the helm for the sake of its own power and profit.

## FACTION

Such self-interested behavior was anticipated by the American Founders. They knew that human beings are naturally more eager to pursue their private good than the good of the whole. Thus, they worried that factious behavior would paralyze and corrupt the politics of the new nation, creating unnecessary divisions and imposing unjust burdens on the general public. Since the days of ancient Greece and Rome, faction had been understood to be a particular danger to republics and the best argument against the adoption of popular government. And, indeed, if the best that could be expected from republics was an unceasing battle for preeminence among their leading factions, republican government would have very little to recommend it.

Convinced, however, that a government founded upon the consent of the governed, led by men chosen by their peers, and pursuing the common good was, in fact, both right and possible, the American Founders analyzed this problem and came up with at least a part of a solution. James Madison summarized their conclusions on the origins of faction in *Federalist* 10: Their causes are "sown in the nature of man"—especially in his fallible judgment, his selfish regard for his own financial interest, and the unavoidable diversity of abilities to acquire wealth. Nevertheless, the Founders believed that the geographic extent of the American republic, the constitutional division between federal and state powers, the establishment of a bicameral Congress, and the system of checks and balances could prevent or contain this human tendency's worst effects. There were, in other words, some ways of structuring the regime that encouraged or tolerated faction less than others.

But they did not rely *merely* on the structure of the regime to mitigate the problem of faction—on what Madison elsewhere called "parchment barriers." Men create factions; men run the governments that are influenced by factions. Thus, with equal importance, they also insisted on the reality of a common good grounded in true principles of justice, in the hope and expectation that the American people would see that seeking special powers and privileges was not only wrong because it was dangerous; it was dangerous because it was wrong.

If we are to understand the depths of the problem with our contemporary politics we must recapture this understanding of the immorality of all our attempts to live at the expense of others. It is one thing to differ over the means by which the common good will be attained; it is another to fight for the political power to secure our own private good. I believe that lower taxes and fewer regulations are in the best interest of all Americans; you think otherwise. We can't both be right, but our difference may be honest and respectable. However, if I want lower taxes and fewer regulations merely for my own gain and you want the opposite for yours, then, dress up our arguments as we may, there is nothing either honest *or* respectable about any of them. We must not turn a blind eye upon political parties or movements that seek the good of their adherents at the expense of the rest. It will not do to look indifferently at interest groups seeking to shape law to their own advantage or the divisive effects of identity politics. Following the example of the Founders, we cannot make peace with the injustice of factions.

## JUSTICE

For at least three generations, however, American universities have labored to convince the public that there is no alternative to the sort of politics the Founders abhorred. Since the publication of political scientist Harold Lasswell's 1936 book, *Who Gets What, When, and How*, American government textbooks have taught that politics is merely concerned with the distribution of society's goods. In this view, the nation is a warehouse with a certain inventory of goods ready to be loaded onto whichever truck can connive to secure a spot at the loading dock. Here, it may truly be said that the personal is political and the political is personal. In fact, the warehouse metaphor breaks down because there is nothing that is intrinsically outside the warehouse, including the trucks and drivers. Everything of earthly value is available for distribution - and every distribution is provisional, lasting only until the next moment's scramble for positioning. The natural response to such a politics is the sort of thing that one observes every day: a hospital that promotes Michelle Obama and triples her salary two months after her husband becomes a US Senator, corporations getting on the "right side" of political issues to avoid trouble with regulators, and a thousand other little (or great) acts of corruption or self-protection.

This is not the definition of politics with which our nation began. Following an ancient tradition, the Founders understood politics to be a branch of moral philosophy. Politics for them, as for Aristotle, was the "science . . . of the good for man." Thus Madison stated briefly: "Justice is the end of government." If government has an end—an ultimate purpose—then not just any distribution of whatever to whomever, whenever and however, will do. One policy may advance the cause of justice; another is only "an improper or wicked project." To be "value neutral" and therefore indifferent between the two is to rob politics of any value at all. *Republican* politics, at least, insists that there is a difference between the just and the unjust that cannot be reduced to a matter of individual or group perspective. Factions form, as Madison argued, as the result of differences in *perceived* interests. We need not conclude, however, that *true* justice varies with one's perception of it or give up on the notion that there is an objective standard of right. The Founders, in sum, would not allow the fact of faction to become the moral justification for factious activity. Theirs was no golden age of man in his innocency. But it was a time when factious corruption was shameful, not normal; delegitimized, not institutionalized.

How does this help to resolve the problem of faction? Obviously, an insistence on the reality of justice does not directly prevent any interest group from pursuing its ignoble schemes. But neither is it thereby powerless. There is something in all of us that makes it impossible entirely to suppress our inherent knowledge of natural right. And yet habit and custom, united with natural moral lassitude, can practically negate its effect on our actual behavior. There is no reason to expect those who have been taught that politics is merely a contest for the accumulation of goods and power to follow anything other than the dictates of their narrow self-interest. Here, as elsewhere, low expectations are usually met. But call a man to something higher, insisting that the justice he knows is the justice he lives, and one makes it more difficult for him to let himself slide back into the pit of factious intrigue.

The American Founders understood the depravity of man and built a government for men, rather than angels. But they also understood that men ought to be better than they are and that the ubiquity of evil does not turn it into good. They would not, like the modern sociologist, define deviancy down until they had reached the lowest common denominator of human wretchedness. Instead, they insisted on the existence and obligation of moral principles measured against which *their own* actions would be found wanting and the necessity in politics, as in the rest of life, of striving to close that gap.

## JUSTICE AND INTEREST

Niccolo Machiavelli famously argued in *The Prince* that the ancient principles of justice condemn the few who try to live by them to being trampled by the rest. Confronted with a similar argument, Socrates had argued that it is still better to be just, since the just man preserves the purity of his soul. As de Tocqueville noted, nineteenth century Americans took a different tack. Rather than argue for the goodness of justice, they sought to establish that justice pays off—that it is the best policy. As practical as this approach might appear to be—then and now—it is insufficient for the purpose of restraining factious political behavior.

According to this principle of "self-interest rightly understood," respect for the rights of others—in business contracts, matters of conscience, or politics—was necessary to produce respect for one's own rights. Although it would seem best for a person to be the one individual breaking the rules while all the rest obey, one could not rationally expect others to acquiesce in this arrangement, making mutual forbearance the more reasonable second choice of all. This is especially true in a popular government where one may move very quickly from political predator to political prey—as they say in Washington: "If you're not at the table, you're on the menu." While there is nothing noble in this mere *modus vivendi*, it may have the practical advantage of producing something like just behavior among those who recognize its sensibility.

There are dangers, however, in relying on self-interest, however "rightly understood," to protect individual rights. For one, there is the very real possibility that the rights themselves may seem to be only an expression of the desires of men, rather than the real gift of their Creator. One may begin to wonder, for example, if the right to life is only something that interested men would like to have, rather than an objective reality. It is a short and easy path to concluding that all rights are the creation of men, who seek only to protect themselves from others they fear might be more powerful.

The greater danger in such an approach is its elevation of selfish action to the status of high moral good. None of us requires much inducement to pursue this course. And while self-interested behavior might be endorsed for the good results it is expected to produce, one must consider that calculations based upon individual pleasure and pain are notoriously subjective and temporary. When someone tells me that it is in my interest (at least in the long run) to respect the rights of others, I may often quite reasonably reply that *not* respecting their rights is to my immediate benefit. What if that benefit is great and tangible? What if the remainder of my life is short (and how could I know otherwise)? What if I believe my position of power is secure? In other words, even if this is true for most people most of the time or even for all people given enough time, it does not follow that it is true for *me, right now*. We all have an interest in the security of our property. But what if I want that music, video, or software for free—and can get it right now? We all have an interest in safety on the roads. But what if I'm late for an important appointment? We all have an interest in keeping as much of our paycheck as possible. But what if a special government program provides me with great personal benefits while spreading the costs among one hundred million taxpayers? We all have an interest in protecting human life. But what if someone tells me my life-threatening disease can be cured through research where only a few embryos are destroyed?  In such cases and many more there is little hope that an appeal to long-term self-interest will be an adequate substitute for a truly compelling moral argument.

## DISTRIBUTIVE "JUSTICE"

Founders like James Madison knew better than their nine-teenth century successors: they insisted that some political actions were simply "improper or wicked" in and of themselves. It was the very nature of the scheme, its intrinsic principle, that made it objectionable, not the mere fact that those who benefited from it today might be the victims to-morrow. It is helpful for us, in light of our contemporary politics, to consider just what those "improper or wicked" projects were: "a rage for paper money, for an abolition of debts, for an equal division of property . . . ."

Madison's list of damnable projects does not shock us today. We have grown rather accustomed to a perpetually inflating currency, government intervention in the relation-ship between debtor and creditor, and a tax system designed first to produce certain social and economic outcomes and only second some quantity of necessary revenue. Thus, it may be worthwhile to restate the reasons such projects were so strongly condemned by men like Madison. A "rage for paper money" was more than a desire for a currency easier to transport and trade than gold. It was grounded in the desire to use political means to alter the value and distribu-tion of wealth – to elevate the debtor at the expense of the creditor. The "abolition of debts" was only a more extreme form of the same thing; the "equal division of property" takes the principle to its logical conclusion. What Madison was objecting to, then, was the use of political power to di-rect private property to those with the political means of acquiring it. It was the presumption that nothing was given in the distribution of property produced by the cumulative effects of free decisions to buy and sell. It was the fact that such laws draw all things within the public sphere and leave a man with no opportunity for the "pursuit of happiness" outside it. It was the self-evident injustice of each scheme.

There is, as Richard Weaver put it, a "metaphysical" link between effort and reward. A young child readily comprehends that he has a better claim to the dollar he earned by raking leaves than to the dollar his sister earned doing the same. Of course, he might very well like to have both dollars, especially if the matchbox car he wants costs $1.99, but he can see that there is no reason why the second dollar should be his, even if, in some moments, he is prepared to wrestle it out of her hands. The temptation to use power as a shortcut to wealth does not disappear when one's desires have moved on to items like homes and SUVs. Nor does the argument against it. Although the denial of the link between effort and reward is evident in many contemporary policies, both the injustice and folly of such attempts can perhaps be best illustrated by examining the behavior of the key actors in the subprime mortgage crisis.

## MORTGAGE MELTDOWN

Three principal groups of people were responsible for the financial crisis that emerged in full force in September, 2008: first, the political leaders who imposed their social agendas upon the nation's mortgage market (through Fanny Mae and Freddy Mac especially), ensuring that mortgages would be available to those who could not afford them; second, those who applied for loans they had no intention or means of paying back; third, those who, at every rung on the ladder, took advantage of government guarantees (explicit or implicit) to write (or resell, securitize, etc.) mortgages divorced from the financial realities of the mortgagor. All three sought to sever the link between effort and reward on behalf of private interests and at the expense of the whole.

The politicians used their power to benefit favored groups, placing the financial risk and now imposing the financial consequences upon the general taxpayer. The lenders (and their cohorts) essentially did the same thing, but were their own favored group. A simple question identifies the problem: If they had had to assume all the *risk* in order to receive all the reward from the loans they made, would they have acted in the same way? Of course not. The American public bore the risk, while individuals and firms reaped the benefits. No different, ultimately, was the behavior of the borrowers. The immediate impression they must have had was that it was only a big, impersonal bank (with lots of money) that stood to lose if they defaulted on their mortgage—and, if the bank was willing to lend, why should they refuse to borrow? However, since the bank had already insured itself against any risk, the real loser turned out to be those who ultimately insured the insurers—here too, the American public.

There are two essential conclusions to draw from this painful experience. First, all three groups unjustly imposed involuntary burdens on some in order to grant unearned benefits to others. We must have moral clarity on this point. Second, the size and scope of the calamity this immoral behavior caused was the direct result of the actions of the political leaders who made private vice a public problem. This is the fundamental point that the Obama Administration misses in its demagogic crusade against bankers.

One would have to be naive to expect men to forego opportunities for easy gain. But a vicious disposition would have found little opportunity for action in this case (and even then with only private consequences) if the government had not imposed an artificial system of costs and benefits on the mortgage market. Political injustice brings consequences individual injustices can rarely equal. Private vice wounds; public vice kills. It is precisely at this point, then, where one must be most vigilant. It is precisely at this point where a republic must guard itself against accepting wicked projects of political money-making as "business as usual."

Our ruling class has, unfortunately, not learned this lesson. Bipartisan legislative solutions that impose new requirements on lenders or borrowers without changing the underlying structure of the system—including the premises that it is the government's responsibility to expand the access of favored groups to mortgages indefinitely and that certain banks and related institutions are "too big to fail"—only guarantee another crash. What is most striking about the bill passed in July, 2010, is that the principal point of negotiation among Democrat and Republican leaders appears to have been only which guarantees and which advantages would be granted to whom—who gets what, when, and how. That the American public remains on the hook for the mess that follows is understood by all, whatever the sound bites and press releases may say (just ask Moody's Investors Service). In the spirit of this, just as the last of the "big seven" banks paid back their bailout funds, President Obama convened a meeting to urge leaders from the largest financial institutions to make an "extraordinary commitment" to rebuilding the American economy by ratcheting up loans to individuals and small businesses. Since there is obviously no need to cajole bankers into loaning money to people who present a reasonable credit risk, this can only be seen as another government attempt to push the lending market beyond its natural bounds.

Even more troubling was the Obama Administration's Christmas Eve, 2009, announcement pledging unlimited aid to Fannie Mae and Freddy Mac (above the $400 billion already available) with Treasury department control of both into (presidential election year) 2012. The problems with this decision are representative of the worst qualities of the administration's domestic program. First is the obvious fiscal irresponsibility in making any such open-ended commitment. Then there is the creeping permanence of the government's takeover of the US mortgage market, more than half of which is linked to Fannie Mae or Freddy Mac. Not only is this one more area of American life that has been drawn fully into the public sphere by President Obama, but it brings with it multitudinous opportunities for manipulation of that market for political or venal purposes (anyone want to bet against a 2012 housing bubble?). Lastly, and most immediately to the point, this only reinforces the notion that behind every Fannie Mae and Freddy Mac mortgage is the US taxpayer, ready to take the hit for the negligence of the directors and politicians.

The most important applications of the lessons of this experience go far beyond the particulars of the mortgage market. To reach them, we must understand what is really wrong here. It is not, ultimately, the size of the price that Americans (and others) are paying. Similar behavior with only one-tenth or one-thousandth the consequences would be equally wrong. What is really wrong is the principle that one can use government power to enrich oneself at the expense of others, receiving a reward unconnected with any corresponding effort. I cannot reasonably object to the actions of the principal players in this crisis unless I foreswear the principle upon which they acted. I cannot object, in other words, unless I reject the factious behavior from which I benefit—the special programs, regulations, tax benefits I enjoy—as much as the factious behavior from which I suffer. In the absence of this, I am only one more person ready to contribute his share to the next crisis—soon to come so long as the government continues to indemnify bad behavior and the interested many to endorse it.

## CONCLUSION

The iconoclastic essayist Albert Jay Nock wrote that there were really only two ways to make money: by economic means or by political means. The first depends upon individual effort and voluntary exchange; the second applies collective power at the point of the sword. Of course, as other parts of this work demonstrate, a full understanding of political justice involves many questions unrelated to wealth and property. But if we would attempt to understand again what it means to be citizens of a republic, we might begin where Founders like Madison started: with a rejection of all "wicked or improper" projects using political means for selfish ends and with the inculcation of public virtue to limit, however imperfectly, the harms of private vice.

# 5

# Lawfulness

*"emancipating slaves, or enslaving freemen"*

—ABRAHAM LINCOLN,
"THE PERPETUATION OF OUR POLITICAL INSTITUTIONS,"
JANUARY 27, 1838

WHEN FORMER Speaker of the House Nancy Pelosi was asked by a reporter about the source of Congress's constitutional authority to require individuals to purchase health insurance, she responded: "Are you serious? Are you serious?"—and then moved on to the next question. Lest there be any doubt about her meaning, her press spokesman told the reporter, "You can put this on the record. That is not a serious question." Judging by their lawsuits and referenda results, a number of states plainly think otherwise. At least in one sense, however, Speaker Pelosi was right. It is not clear that anyone with whom she would take counsel (or too many others in our ruling class) considers the Constitution an impediment to whatever those who hold government power wish to do. Nevertheless, this is neither more nor less than the negation of constitutional republicanism, which rests, in the United States, on the principle that the *Constitution* defines the powers of our government, rather than our individual perceptions of what is desirable or expedient. This is our common protection against injustice and our common consolation against political despair. To lose an election is not to lose all—so long as the Constitution binds all. As a result, the *first and most important question* for any leader to answer must be: Are your actions authorized by the Constitution? To respond to such a question as Speaker Pelosi did is to say: I can do to you whatever I can get away with—and to teach the rest of us to act on the same principle whenever we get the chance. This is not a republic, but a state of war.

## THE LIBERATOR AND THE EMANCIPATOR

Although the American Founders recognized the immorality of slavery, they, and the two generations that succeeded them, struggled to find the right way to do away with it. And yet throughout this period, there were any number of available means of ending slavery: individual families might make the private decision to emancipate their own slaves; state governments could abolish slavery within their borders; an amendment to the US Constitution could abolish it throughout the nation. But, of course, none of these approaches brought any certainty of success. Some slaveholders, like George Washington, would free their slaves; others, like Thomas Jefferson, would not. While Pennsylvania adopted a plan for gradual emancipation, Kentucky demurred. Until three-quarters of the states agreed, no constitutional amendment could be approved. The difficultly was that each depended upon the consent of (at least some portion of) the slaveholders. But then why not abolish slavery with the brute force of the national government, supported by the northern majority? Since only force justified slavery, no slaveholder could object in principle to using it to *end* slavery. Radical abolitionists like William Lloyd Garrison saw no reason to hesitate: "No matter, though, to effect it, every party should be torn by dissensions, every sect dashed into fragments, the national compact dissolved, the land filled with the horrors of a civil and a servile war—still, slavery must be buried in the grave of infamy, beyond the possibility of a resurrection." Neither the slaveholder *nor* the radical abolitionist saw any principle that might be weighed against the good that it preferred.

Abraham Lincoln, however, knew that the same raw power that could free slaves might just as easily enslave free men. An appeal to force, beyond the law and the Constitution, put more at risk than the illegitimate property of the slave owners. Arbitrary power, in the hands of the majority as much as in those of a despot, negates the rule of law—essential to a republic. Lincoln argued that *despite* slavery's evil, temporary toleration of it was required because obeying the law and the Constitution is a matter of justice too—and protects the rights of all Americans. This is how Clint Eastwood's character in *Hang 'Em High* reasoned when he risked his life to bring three cattle rustlers to justice, instead of letting the rest of his posse lynch them. This is why honest men keep their word to scoundrels—and why each of us must abide by the limits of the Constitution.

## NECESSITY

William Lloyd Garrison's approach to abolishing slavery is one example of a general class of arguments that has grown increasingly common in our politics—the appeal to necessity. The basic contours of the argument are easy to describe: a crisis exists in some area of our social or political life; the dangers of inaction are (projected to be) catastrophic; any action (claimed to be) necessary to avoid the catastrophe is required and, therefore, right. Garrison's argument, if ultimately dangerous, was certainly superior to most contemporary appeals to necessity since it was grounded in the deep moral wrong being done at every moment to millions of actual Americans. Compare that with the various "crises" that have supposedly been upon us over the last several decades in just one area: the environment. In the 1970s, we had to act *now* to stave off a coming ice age, the apocalyptic effects of runaway population growth, and the imminent exhaustion of numerous natural resources. During the 1980s we had to act *now* to prevent a post-war nuclear winter, the uncontrolled growth of toxic waste sites, and the imminent exhaustion of numerous natural resources. In the 1990s, we had to act *now* to close the expanding hole in the ozone layer, save the disappearing wetlands, and prevent the imminent exhaustion of numerous natural resources. Today, we have to act *now* to stop global warming—and the imminent exhaustion of numerous natural resources. Each time, the "experts" speak gravely about the threat, rally the ambitious, idealistic, and credulous to their cause, and propose various draconian measures that are guaranteed to do at least one thing: increase their own prominence and research funding (as the exposure of the "Climategate" emails and data made clear). But while our cynicism concerning such crises may be well-merited, this is not a sufficient response to this type of argument as a whole. To begin to fill out what is missing, we must restate the case for a careful adherence to the law in general and the Constitution in particular. While this principle may lack some of the emotional appeal of Garrison's (or the environmentalist's) call to action, we would be foolish to allow this to obscure its real goodness.

The opening chapters of this work present a moral framework that asks much of republican citizens. First, they must acknowledge their fundamental equality with their fellow citizens, regardless of the division of physical, economic, or political power among them. Second, they must recognize the existence of ethical limits on all human action and apply them in the public sphere. The principle of lawfulness is one of the most important applications of these two ideas. It establishes a rule of equity between those who have power and those who do not—all are bound by the common law of the community. A proper law speaks indifferently to the high and the low, the rich and the poor, the sophisticated and the simple. It is also an excellent tutor in teaching the moral limits of politics. It reminds me that I am not autonomous. If I must obey the law and the Constitution, then there are some political actions beyond my power. I then ask: why? As I investigate the reason of the law, I am inevitably instructed in natural right. A well-framed law works out the rational limits of human behavior. Even a bad law forces me to give reasons for judging it so. And if there is a reason that the law is bad, then there must be an underlying moral principle that is as binding upon me as it is upon the erring lawmakers. Thus, a commitment to lawfulness is both derived from and a protection of the first principles for republican citizenship.

There are other important goods generated by strict adherence to the law, including the stability that it promotes. Among other things, this allows people the freedom to pursue projects that may take time to mature, confident in the expectation that the rules under which they began their labors will continue until their conclusion. This principle is so important to the pursuit of private enterprise that free market economist F.A. Hayek argued that in most cases it is more important that the law be stable and obeyed than that the law be good.

Danger, however, is not found only in cases where laws are literally ignored or new rules extra-constitutionally imposed. Even when the formal legislative process is followed, a dramatic change in the law and the established expectations it has produced can have similarly troubling effects. President Obama, building upon actions taken in the last months of the Bush Administration, has spent extraordinary amounts of money and imposed constitutionally-dubious financial regulations in the name of avoiding economic disaster. Nevertheless, the American economy has ended up in worse shape that the administration had projected *if they had done nothing.* Is it possible to spend hundreds of billions of dollars and make things worse? It certainly is, as a variety of economists have shown. But even if, after all the laughable "jobs saved or created" claims are exposed, there is some net positive impact from the stimulus bill and all the rest (the big benefits always "coming soon"), the administration's destabilizing interventions into the health care, energy, and financial markets must certainly have greatly overwhelmed it.

Why would anyone hire an extra worker in an environment where massive new health care mandates (with penalties for noncompliance) not only overhang the national economy, but change daily, according to the political needs of their advocates? Even with a bill in place, there is little reason to believe that the law is anywhere close to settled especially when one considers its political insecurity, on the one hand, and the vast areas of regulatory discretion it has opened up for enterprising bureaucrats and self-serving politicians, on the other. Then there's the ongoing uncertainty about how and to what degree Congress and, especially, the EPA will attempt to force energy prices up. And how, despite all the president's jawboning, will entrepreneurs get the loans they need when a snake-bit financial sector is daily threatened with new, ever-more-draconian taxes and regulations? If you can't find credit, don't know what your labor costs will be, and have reason to believe that your utility bill is about to skyrocket, you aren't going to expand your business.

Besides providing the stability necessary for enterprise, fidelity to the law also reinforces the good man's allegiance to republican institutions. There are few things more demoralizing to the law-abiding man than to find that the actions of those who have won the latest election have ruined all that his careful planning and tireless toil have built—or that the government no longer can be counted on to take his side against the lawless. What does it say about the state of our republic when Arizona has to pass a law and commit its own resources to enforce existing federal immigration policy—

and then finds itself demonized and sued by the very administration whose neglect had all but forced its hand? A noble citizen's love of self-government may overcome many such disappointments, but could we wonder if eventually a limit might be reached? We may not expect him to reconsider the merits of the eighteenth century monarchy, but the cold comforts of the systematized bureaucratic state may begin to look comparatively attractive.

A strong presumption in favor of following the law and the Constitution—especially by those in power—is, thus, fundamental to republican politics. Nevertheless, this principle has its limits in the case of *real* necessity. Abraham Lincoln faced such a situation early in the Civil War. Confederate troops fired on Fort Sumter on April 12, 1861. In the normal course of events, the Congress elected in 1860 would not have met for the first time until December, 1861. Even a special session of Congress could not convene until July 4, 1861. By then, the Union and the Constitution that held it together might be lost forever. Lincoln thus judged that it was appropriate for him to undertake certain war measures as commander in chief (especially the suspension of the writ of habeas corpus) that were arguably or explicitly within the legislature's constitutional sphere until the Congress could meet. A strict adherence to (a narrow interpretation of) every part of the Constitution he had sworn to protect would, in this case, hazard the loss of all the further good it might secure. Thus, Lincoln asked the Congress, "Are all the laws but one to go unexecuted and the Government itself go to pieces lest that one be violated?" Nothing short of our nation's deepest crisis would induce Lincoln to contravene (if he did)—even temporarily, openly, and revocably—one jot or tittle of the Constitution. Like the principle of unalterable adherence to the law itself, the Constitution could not be used to destroy the very rights it was established to protect.

We must acknowledge, as Lincoln did, that even truly necessary (and temporary) actions beyond the law or the Constitution are dangerous. Power, once assumed, is not easily relinquished. It astonished the world when George Washington, both at the end of the Revolutionary War and at the conclusion of his two terms as president, freely gave up his power and went back to his farm. Lincoln himself was in the process of giving up war-time powers when he was assassinated. But most people do not relinquish the scepter once they've grasped it. Nor is there ever a shortage of those willing to use a "crisis" as an excuse for grabbing power or actions done in moments of highest danger as precedents for similar behavior in more tranquil times. As a result, the federal government has grown most often through the indefinite perpetuation of powers and programs assumed or established during times of crisis. That is why it is so important to be skeptical of crisis legislation and to insist that temporary measures, truly required by extraordinary times, be temporary.

## "A RATIONALE"

Frequent acquiescence to appeals to necessity inevitably makes expediency the rule of politics. Whatever may be said on behalf of this principle (or the similar ethical rule of utility) as a general guide to action, it is unquestionably the case that it is antithetical to the core principles of our regime. The Declaration of Independence states that it is the government's responsibility to protect individual natural rights even when this is inconvenient to the general multitude of citizens. The Constitution establishes fixed limits to the powers of the federal government. The Founders rejected utility as the moral basis for our regime because the principle of maximizing collective pleasure does not place any ultimate limits on individual or collective human action. Even with the best of intentions, it often turns in to an assertion of the right of the majority to dictate terms to the rest. Thus, especially in light of our present rush to do "whatever it takes" to address a multitude of issues, it is essential that we insist that the powers of government be defined by our principles rather than our principles defined by the powers of government.

The Obama Administration, unfortunately, will not be easily convinced. One relatively small example illustrates the problem. Since the breakdown of the financial-services industry, it has been the desire of many to limit executive compensation within that field as a whole. While it may be reasonable to impose broad-ranging federal oversight on those firms that voluntarily accept government bailout funds, there is no logical or constitutional basis for establishing a general pay scale for any privately-owned business. Nevertheless, our bloated and over-muscled government has many non-legislative ways to turn the will of the ruling class into the rule for all. in this case, the Federal Reserve and the SEC, among other agencies, have been considered "available." The principle is clear: Whatever is expedient must be lawful. This is not an isolated instance or even one of a number of examples that have multiplied by happenstance. It is, in fact, the logical unfolding of President Obama's long-held views on the Constitution, now become the ruling principle of American politics.

Near the end of the presidential campaign, a recording was released from a 2001 appearance on public radio by then-state senator and sometime constitutional law professor Obama. He suggested that it was inappropriate to call the (liberal) Earl Warren Supreme Court "radical" since it had not transgressed "essential constraints that were placed by the founding fathers in the Constitution, at least as it's been interpreted . . . ." On the other hand, he suggested that "any three of us sitting here could come up with a rationale for bringing ['redistributive'] economic change through the courts." A "rationale," as defined here, is the exact opposite of a responsible constitutional argument—an excuse for using the Constitution as a vehicle for a pre-determined political agenda. A broad phrase—"equal protection," "general welfare," or the like—is ripped entirely out of its linguistic and historical context and infused with whatever meaning is necessary to reach the required result. To submit to the Constitution in truth is to read it like *neither* Chief Justice Warren nor Professor Obama, but to frame one's political agenda according to its design, rather than the reverse.

President Obama's constitutional reasoning suggests a flexibility with language and an approach to politics that is incompatible with the principle of lawfulness. There is no ultimate difference between ignoring the Constitution as a rule for political action and making it mean whatever three willful people around a table want it to mean. In either case, the Constitution's restrictions on government power are meaningless.

## CRISIS POLITICS

The most remarkable fact of the present economic crisis has been how quickly the ruling class (and, for a time, large portions of the public) seized upon and then actively promoted measures entirely at odds with our political heritage. "You never want a serious crisis to go to waste," said President Obama's chief of staff, Rahm Emanuel, shortly after the election—and he meant it. One day the United States was a nation of publicly-traded, privately-held (and privately-run) businesses. The next day, the federal government was part-owner and full director of some of our country's largest corporations. One moment (July 28, 2008) the Bush Administration was being criticized for its projected record $482 billion 2009 budget deficit and general fiscal irresponsibility. The next moment, President Obama was shepherding a stimulus package through Congress that, in conjunction with the weakening economy and numerous Obama-endorsed or -directed bailouts, led to a $1.4 trillion deficit for 2009, within range of the *total* deficit for the eight years of the Bush Administration. After the president decided it was time to get serious about the deficit, he proposed a $3.8 trillion 2010 budget—with a $1.6 trillion deficit. That is like spending $100,000 on your $58,000 salary. How long can you get away with that?

All this was done because, first the Bush Administration and then the Obama Administration told us, there really was no choice. We were on the verge of (or in the early stages of) a worldwide economic collapse. Spend $700 billion buying "toxic assets" from banks or we would lose our homes and savings. Spend another $787 billion to stimulate the economy or prepare for breadlines and Hoovervilles. Bailout Chrysler (again) and General Motors or both would go bankrupt, with devastating consequences across numerous industries. Who could ignore such calamitous predictions? The (approved) experts had all the computer models and four-color graphs to prove them. Congress acceded; the money was printed. And then strange things began to happen: *zero* billion dollars was spent buying bad debt. Instead, the government purchased a controlling interest, voluntarily or not, in leading banks—but the world banking system did not collapse. Only $88 billion of the stimulus funds was spent by mid-May, but the beginning of renewed economic growth was all of a sudden projected for the third quarter (July-September), 2009. Unemployment, which we were warned might climb as high as 9 percent if the stimulus bill was not approved, reached 10.2 percent anyway in October (2009). Meanwhile, GM and Chrysler got their money—and bankruptcy too. The results were simultaneously better and worse than our experts projected.

But perhaps we should have realized at the first that the administration's predictions and their accuracy were really beside the point. After all, Rahm Emanuel had warned us that the Obama Administration would use the economic turmoil to its best political advantage. Thus, as noted earlier, every item on its agenda was framed as a necessary step to "get America back to work"—from a government healthcare takeover (cutting employer costs) to energy taxes and heavy-handed measures to counteract "climate change" (green jobs!).

Judged according to their impact on the national economy, the results of the government's many interventions are not impressive. But judged by what one may reasonably suspect is their ultimate purpose—the permanent expansion of federal power—they are quite remarkable. The US government, after all, now has a revolving fund with which to buy shares of businesses in targeted industries, with all the consequences for intimate oversight and regulation that follow. The stimulus funds gave every member of Congress something (or ten things) to tout in the fall campaign. Federal agencies, which nearly missed the crisis (putting together their spending plans in May, 2009), still have tens or hundreds of billions of dollars to spread around among their friends and partisans. Two-thirds of the US auto industry has become a joint venture between the federal government and the United Auto Workers, with the former determined to produce its preferred fleet of cars and the latter now delighted to find itself on both sides of the negotiating table. Lawlessness too has had its day: bankruptcy rules have been rewritten; contracts have been broken; limited powers have been given unlimited effect. The crisis surely has *not* been wasted. The government has its power, the experts have their influence, the insiders have their money, and the people have the bill—and whatever is left of the rule of law.

## CONCLUSION

The Civil War was the tragic outcome of the lawlessness of both the radical abolitionists and the southern slaveholders. The price the nation paid was nearly all that Garrison was willing to hazard: a terrible civil war, the division of parties and churches—but not the destruction of the Constitution.

Confounding the champions of slavery and abolition alike, Lincoln, as commander-in-chief, first, as an act of war, freed only the slaves in rebelling territories unreconciled to the union after one hundred days of prior notice. But since the war gave him no more power over slavery in the loyal states than he had when he took office, Lincoln then promoted nationwide emancipation through the regular means of constitutional amendment, a process completed shortly after his death. The slaves were then permanently free—and the principles of republican government secure for another day. If *we* willingly allow the perpetual claims of "crisis" to trump every legal, moral, and constitutional norm, freeing today's "slaves" will only mean empowering government to do whatever it wants to (formerly) free men—and those who follow *us* will have a much less desirable inheritance.

# 6

## Prudence

*"the course of ultimate extinction"*

—Abraham Lincoln,
A House Divided," June 16, 1858

THE EARLIEST test for the 2012 Republican presidential contenders didn't take place in Iowa or New
Hampshire, but in the unlikely location of upstate New
York. The November, 2009, three-way race to represent the
twenty-third congressional district of New York turned into
a trial of Republican Party loyalty and adherence to conservative principles after Sarah Palin endorsed Conservative
Party candidate Doug Hoffman two weeks before the election. Potential presidential contenders Rick Santorum and
Tim Pawlenty quickly followed suit. On the other hand,
Newt Gingrich took a very public stand for party loyalty
and deference to local leaders in supporting Republican
candidate Dede Scozzafava, despite her generally liberal
views. Meanwhile, Mitt Romney and Mike Huckabee split
the difference: Romney announced that he was *not* endors-
ing Scozzafava; Huckabee sided with Hoffman—but only
after Scozzafava had left the race. While Hoffman's narrow
loss to Democrat Bill Owens (after Scozzafava dropped out
and endorsed Owens) left all candidates room to justify

their position in this particular contest, the deeper questions it exposed about party and principle are an enduring part of republican politics. How should the risk of defeat be measured against the purity of a cause? When is half a political loaf (or less) better than none? And, more deeply, how, both morally and strategically, are significant reformations of our politics and policy to be brought about in an ideologically-divided republic?

## A DIVIDED HOUSE

Abraham Lincoln argued, at the beginning of the 1858 Illinois Senate campaign, that the United States was a "house divided against itself" on the issue of slavery. In response, his opponent, Stephen Douglas, asked a very obvious question: Why was this any more the case in 1858 than at any other time since 1780 (when Massachusetts became the first American state to abolish slavery)? Douglas argued that, since the United States had been a mixture of free and slave states for nearly eighty years, there was no reason to think that this condition could not continue indefinitely. Lincoln's response was two-fold. First, he argued that the fact that the Union had not hitherto collapsed did not mean that the division over slavery was safe. Each time the incorporation of new slave states into the nation was contemplated or attempted, sectional strife had threatened to break up the Union. That this had been avoided by prudent actions like the great compromises of 1820 and 1850 did not mean that the wells of political comity ran infinitely deep. This was especially true because of the second point Lincoln raised: the breakdown of the political consensus that had existed from the nation's founding down to 1854 that slavery was wrong and in "the course of ultimate extinction." So long as that consensus existed, Lincoln himself was content to let the abolition of slavery come when it may. But that consensus *had* broken down. Douglas had pushed through Congress the Kansas-Nebraska Act in 1854, a law that threatened to expand slavery indefinitely by repealing the Missouri Compromise and allowing American territories to decide for themselves whether they would have slavery—to decide by popular vote whether a man would be free. Now, Lincoln concluded, the central principle of the American regime— that "all men are created equal"—was in danger. If Douglas's principle prevailed, the United States might, for the first time, establish slavery where it did not already exist. It might begin to accept slavery as a permanent and even central part of the regime (as the southern confederacy would). Thus Lincoln stood forthrightly against Douglas not, as we have seen, to bring about the immediate abolition of slavery, but to put it back where the Founders placed it: in "the course of ultimate extinction."

The complexity of Lincoln's approach to slavery was difficult for many of his contemporaries (and later historians) to appreciate. Was his willingness to tolerate slavery for a time indicative of a lack of appreciation for its true injustice? Was his rejection of the series of compromise measures proposed by Senator John Crittenden in the midst of the secession crisis of 1860 to 1861 indicative of a covert zeal for violent abolition? The answer to both of these (essentially contradictory) questions was no. Lincoln would never make peace with slavery's gross violation of natural rights, but he was willing to compromise on any practical point so long as it was consistent with the fact that slavery was wrong and therefore ought not to be extended. Just as Ronald Reagan, in his dangerous (to the *New York Times*) and unsophisticated (to the Kissinger-Nixon "realists") way, insisted that communism was "evil," Lincoln constantly declared the gross immorality of slavery. Just as Reagan was prepared to apply moral, economic, and military pressure on the Soviet Union until it fell, but would not risk all in a direct attack on the nation, Lincoln hoped to consolidate and extend the free territory of the nation until slavery withered way, while avoiding a direct confrontation with the south. Thus, he proposed a constitutional amendment that would have provided compensation to slave owners in states that abolished slavery as late as 1900, but would not agree to an amendment recognizing the permanent right to slavery in the southern territories. Lincoln, in sum, would accept any reasonable means adapted to the just end, but reject whatever made that end more difficult to achieve or conceded the moral principle at the heart of it. It is this right appreciation of means and ends that defines prudent republican statesmanship.

## REPUBLICAN MEANS AND ENDS

In any system of popular government, it is necessary to assemble majority coalitions in order to govern. Under our system, such coalitions are primarily constructed before (general) elections in the broad platforms and practical compromises that bring together the disparate elements that make up the two major parties. But the construction of majority coalitions is not the ultimate goal of republican politics. Rather, such coalitions are the means to implementing policy and, ultimately, to realizing a fuller measure of justice, the purpose of government. Here we find the problem. Without the coalition, there is no progress in justice. But the fuller the attempt to realize justice, the more difficult it often is to assemble the coalition. It would (perhaps) be nice if this were not so, but at least as long as there remains a connection between a man's interest and his politics, it will be unreasonable and ineffectual to ignore the central role of compromise in republican politics. Thus it is necessary to understand the contours of proper compromise, as modeled by Lincoln and others, and to cultivate the prudence that is needed to craft the means necessary to accomplish just ends.

## GRANDSTANDING, COMPROMISE, AND CONCESSION

There is something noble in a political defeat that comes from standing on uncompromising principle. And yet there can also be something that is unreal and unserious in the whole exercise. A leader and his followers sleep easily, their consciences clear, while the practical result is the continuation of a policy or the victory of a cause that they are supposed to abhor. If the cause is more than an abstraction, a way to avoid being called a "sell-out" or to establish one's ethical bona fides, there ought to be something unsettling about this. If it is truly an expression of a real desire for justice—justice for actual people—then principled defeat may begin to look like self-absorbed grandstanding.

On the other hand, it is very easy for compromise to begin to look not like a means to justice, but like justice itself, as if bringing people together is the absolute and every other principle is negotiable. "Statesmen" make deals while "politicians" debate. Unfortunately, such deals too often concede essential principles and make important objects more difficult to attain.

The key to understanding the difference between grandstanding and compromise on the one hand and compromise and concession on the other is to recognize the political necessity (and often the moral necessity) of pursuing a long-term goal through a number of intermediate steps. Grandstanders see the goal, but not the steps necessary to reach it, while conceders see steps, but only so haphazardly arranged as to obscure any ultimate goal. A proper compromise maintains contact with both political reality and ultimate ends. It accepts whatever half-measure is available so long as it does not give up the essential principle in the matter or unnecessarily delay its political actualization. In the normal course of affairs, it will not always be easy to distinguish this from these two alternatives. If one cannot accept compromise on just any terms, he may find himself, like the grandstander, losing on principle. If one is willing to accept much less than a whole loaf, he may find himself, like the conceder, making common cause with those with whom he has profound disagreements. But the very fact that he will be in one group on one occasion and the other at a different time, will reveal, to the discerning, an approach to politics in principle different from each.

The easier work of stating these distinctions must give way to the more challenging task of applying them. To do that, consider two areas of policy with distinctly different qualities: abortion, where any compromise seems impossible and likely to require giving up on fundamental principles, and taxation, where almost all compromises seem reasonable so long as tax rates are moving in the right direction.

## ABORTION POLITICS

We have noted the moral and political parallels between our contemporary abortion debate and the earlier American division over slavery. Both involve the definition of personhood and the relationship between weak and strong. Both are bound up with deep and personal interests, apparently non-negotiable moral principles, and controversial Supreme Court decisions. Even the sectional division between north and south that was central to the politics of slavery is not entirely absent in red state/blue state cleavage of abortion politics. Both cases, in sum, seem to involve intractable divisions not amenable to normal republican politics. One would be liable to conclude, then, that justice for the slave and justice for the unborn child were both hopeless causes except for the fact that slavery in America is no more. Time has even given its abolition an air of inevitability. This, however, obscures the great difficulty with which our most discerning statesmen perceived the ultimate means by which that great end would be accomplished. Is it possible, in an analogous way, that our own dim perception of the final steps in the abolition of abortion may, in one hundred years, be overtaken by the presumption that it too was certain to end? Even if we doubt this result, we might ask, in the spirit of Lincoln, what would it take to place abortion "in the course of ultimate extinction?"

The non-negotiable philosophical premise in the fight against slavery was simply that it was wrong—a denial of the humanity and dignity of the slave. For abortion, it must be the same. It will not do to qualify this for the sake of political expediency. What about those who are "personally opposed" to abortion, but willing to tolerate it legislatively? This stance is generally assumed for the sake of not "imposing" one's religious beliefs on others. But what is the special religious premise in opposition to abortion? It certainly can't be that it should be illegal to take a human life. Then it must be that a child is a human being at conception. But one may as easily demonstrate this biologically or philosophically as assert it dogmatically. The question involved is a matter of fact, open to investigation and subject to rational argument. It makes no sense to say that because I am a Christian the child is a human being, but because you are an agnostic he is not. He is, or is not, a human being. And if he is, what does it mean to personally oppose someone taking his life?

There is no more room for compromise in the oft-cited cases of rape or incest. Again, it is simply unreasonable to argue that a child's humanity is determined by the circumstances under which he was conceived. What even limited social privilege would we deny to a child outside the womb simply because he had been conceived incestuously? Could the most important right of all be contingent on such an accidental circumstance (for the child)? If someone were to tell me that he was personally opposed to my murder, but didn't think there was anything for the law to do about it, or thought it should be illegal so long as I hadn't been conceived the wrong way, I think that I would want to know if he was willing to apply these principles to himself. And if not, then I would know that, whatever his stated view on the matter, he had never really embraced the only principle upon which it would be right to oppose abortion at all: All human beings, born and unborn, are objectively entitled to the full protection of the law.

There is one very large impediment to taking even small steps toward having the law embody this principle: Roe v. Wade and the legal framework built up around it. Since 1973, the Supreme Court has asserted that it is unconstitutional to prohibit abortion at any stage of pregnancy if the life or health (including mental health) of the mother is at risk and at any point prior to viability even if they are not. For all practical purposes, this means that no abortion can be legally proscribed (though certain procedural regulations, approvals, and delays have been upheld). As a result, the effort to overturn Roe v. Wade as an unconstitutional judicial imposition cannot be given up—nor need it be. A strong respect for legal precedent is an important part of the rule of law, but a precedent that is antithetical to the philosophical underpinnings of the regime both in its method of reasoning (as argued in chapter 1) and its conclusions (as argued in chapter 2) not only may be, but must be, opposed in order to uphold the more fundamental law.

At this point, one may begin to wonder: Is there any room left for prudent compromise? This is a fair question though we must also recognize that identifying those points upon which we may not compromise is equally necessary. Lincoln could no more concede the rightness of slavery than we the rightness of abortion. Lincoln could no more accede to the principles of the Dred Scott decision than we to the principles of Roe v. Wade. The key compromise on slavery came in the distinction between abolishing it where it already existed and preventing its extension to territories where it didn't. Is there any equivalent for the politics of abortion? Legislatively, laws must be passed that build upon the Born-Alive Infants Protection Act (BAIPA) of 2002. This law, first conceived by Amherst College Professor Hadley Arkes, codified a simple, but essential premise: A child born alive, whether as a result of natural birth, caesarean section, or induced (but failed) abortion, possesses the same legal rights as any other person. In essence, it made birth an objective point after which the legal standing of the child is equal to and distinct from that of the mother. The next logical step is to extend this legal protection back to the point of viability. As with the BAIPA, there need not be any conflict between this law and the argument that human life begins at conception. That I assert the humanity of an eighteen year-old does not mean that I deny the humanity of a six year-old. Thus, with such a law, nothing is conceded philosophically and a point upon which a great many Americans agree—the immorality of late-term abortions— is gained, protecting real human lives.

One of the advantages of the Born-Alive Infants Protection Act was that, in concentrating on the point of birth, it necessitated no confrontation with *Roe*. Further (significant) legal progress on abortion, however, cannot be made without it. The question then becomes: What sort of confrontation should be attempted? In the last few years, South Dakota has narrowly failed in several attempts to ban abortion at all stages of pregnancy. Why not redouble efforts there (or in another similar state) in the hope of having the Supreme Court overturn *Roe* entirely, rather than take the small step we have proposed? There are at least two reasons to take the more limited approach. First, it is much easier for the court to reaffirm *Roe* in the face of a complete ban on abortion than it would be in the case of a law that dealt only with viable unborn children. The court has already declared the point of viability to be legally significant in *Roe* and *Casey*, among other key decisions. Upholding the law we have proposed would only require it to recognize the legal independence of the child from the mother at the point when his physical independence is possible—a conclusion with a common sense plausibility not easily dismissed.

It is important to remember that the Court has always been a careful guardian of its legitimacy and authority. Presenting it with a case that requires a choice between a relatively slight revision of *Roe* and the justification of a legal right to the least defensible instances of abortion is well-calculated to take advantage of this and prepare the ground for further legal progress. This is no guarantee of success— even laws banning partial-birth abortion were judged to be unconstitutional from 2000 to 2007—but in giving the court a legally-defensible alternative to continuing to prop up the tottering framework of abortion extremism, one may reasonably hope to see the beginnings of a return to the court's legal, rather than ideological, consideration of the matter.

The second reason for focusing on smaller confrontations with the abortion legal regime is that these might run parallel to the necessary work of moral suasion in cultivating a political consensus opposing abortion. Since

1994, a majority of Americans (between 51 percent and 63 percent) in every Gallup poll taken has supported either making abortion illegal under all circumstances or in all but a few circumstances. Moreover, for more than thirty years, the percentage of Americans who believe that abortion should be *legal* in all circumstances has been between 22 percent and 34 percent (22 percent in May, 2009). Thus, during the entire post-*Roe* period, between two-thirds and three-quarters of the American people have favored making some abortions illegal. However, over the same period, only 12 percent to 23 percent (23 percent in May, 2009) have supported abolition of abortion altogether. It is quite reasonable to believe that (at least many) people who morally oppose *some* abortions may come to morally oppose *all* abortions, but most of them haven't yet. Prudent abortion legislation can both take that into account and help move public opinion in the right direction through the public discourse that accompanies it.

Two times the South Dakota law fell short of a majority in state-wide referenda. Even, however, if it were to have passed with a small majority (and been able to go into effect without legal challenge), the practical value of the victory would likely have been limited. Abortions in other states and illegal abortions would have substantially reduced the number of actual lives saved. A massive legal and political effort to overturn the law would have immediately followed with a strong likelihood of success. An important change to an important law would have taken place without the political consensus to sustain it.

The legal end of abortion will not be secured by a bare majority in a single election. This will only come when a large portion of the American public is brought to reject all abortions in the way that, during the late 1990s, it came to reject partial-birth abortion. Thus, the most important political work on abortion today is the clear and reasonable presentation of the case against it and the step by step codification of more limited regulations on abortion where such a consensus exists. The resources that might be expended on behalf of premature attempts at final victory would undoubtedly save more lives if devoted to these causes and to person by person care for women in the midst of crisis pregnancies. The moral urgency of the fight against abortion will have the tragic consequence of postponing or lessening its victory if it is not joined with a prudence capable of securing, step by step, the real protection of actual unborn children.

## TAX POLITICS

The strength of the Tea Party movement, initially organized to protest the Obama Administration's early fiscal irresponsibility, indicates that there is something about burdensome taxation that continues to stick in the American craw. Here too it is necessary to understand our means and our ends in order to receive the greatest practical benefit from this powerful grass-roots uprising.

One must not begrudge the federal government the revenue necessary to meet its constitutional responsibilities—an impotent government is no friend to life, liberty, and the pursuit of happiness. Present tax revenues, however, go far beyond this point, making the American people unnecessarily dependent upon the government. Every dollar of mine that makes its way to Washington, even if it eventually ends up back in my pocket, is a dollar over which I lose control—a dollar that achieves someone else's goals rather than mine. This dependency increases all the more when tax revenue is used to provide services that the government has made available only by its hand. The paternalistic state, so antithetical to republican equality, relies upon the stick of high tax rates to create dependency and the carrot of universal benefits to sanitize it. All tax cuts, then, are useful at least in countering this danger. But there is a great need for prudence in determining *how* one cuts taxes because the terms of one tax cut create the context in which the next one will be debated.

The policy of progressive taxation (taxing higher incomes at higher rates) has several unrepublican elements to it. First and foremost, it allows groups to use political power to redistribute the burdens of taxation in their favor. Those in one tax bracket are played off against those in another in a destructive game of "beggar thy neighbor." A universal tax rate, on the other hand, leaves no room for using tax policy to choose winners and losers, but instead reinforces the notion of equality under the law that is the foundation of republican government. Because of this, adopting a universal tax rate would probably do more to inculcate republican habits in the American people than any other single policy change. It would also counter a second troubling consequence of progressive taxation: increasing the sphere of private activity that is influenced by government action. A universal tax rate frees a man from the worry that he or his "group" might be singled out for special hardships. Even if he has no desire to join the soul-deadening scramble to make someone else pay, he cannot be sure that no one else will and so must devote his time or his money to understanding the present tax regime and the contending alternatives that at any given moment are vying to replace it. In a republic, a man's prosperity should not depend upon what his lobbyists are able to do or prevent in Washington D.C. With progressive (loop-hole-filled) taxation, however, this is an inescapable reality, as the unseemly scramble of the labor unions to protect their members from new health insurance taxes demonstrated. Thus, both reducing tax rates and reducing progressivity (and all other forms of differentiated taxation) are important objectives. Neither of these will be easily obtained, but they will become practically impossible without a due measure of prudence.

It is one of the iron laws of American politics that a tax cut proposed by a Republican president or Congress will be characterized (or caricatured) as a plan to benefit the wealthy. It makes no difference if all tax rates are cut, child deductions are increased, or any other measures are included with a disproportionate impact on middle or lower income earners. Part of the reason for this is the connection between taxes and government dependency already discussed. Those who seek to cultivate such dependency must oppose all tax cuts and this sort of argument will almost always be the easiest way to do it. While there may be a number of Joe the Plumbers who object to high tax rates on the wealthy even when they are not (at least at the moment), there is also enough envy to exploit to give the pro-tax movement a fighting chance if it can frame the debate in class terms.

President Bush attempted to counter this argument with a proposal that reduced taxes more at the bottom of the income range than at the top. Just more than a tenth was taken off the top tax rate, which fell (in three stages) from 39.6 percent to 35 percent. A comparable reduction (about a tenth) was made to the three middle rates. The bottom tax bracket was split into two with the lower quarter of the original range now taxed at 10 percent, rather than 15 percent, a decrease of one-third the original rate on the affected income. As a result, the ratio between the top tax rate and the bottom tax rate increased from 2.5 under President Clinton to 3.5 under President Bush. In short, the Bush tax cuts, at least by one obvious measure, made the tax code *more* progressive. The impact of this law was an increase in the percentage of federal income tax revenue generated from top income earners and a corresponding decrease in the percentage of people who pay any net income tax at all. The implications for future tax policy are obvious. The more tax revenue is generated from top income earners, the more any future tax cut will be open to demagogic appeals to envy. How hard will it be to make a perfectly proportional income tax cut look unfair if 60 percent of the tax reduction would go to the top 5 percent of wage earners? The increase in the number of people who pay no net income tax is equally troubling. Here is a growing and powerful potential constituency for the worst sort of class politics with no interest at all in further rate reductions. Thus, while President Bush was able to secure the approval of a tax cut with his small congressional majorities, further progress toward a low and universal tax rate has very likely been made more difficult to achieve. The next genuine tax-cutting president will have to be more careful in expending his political capital for a plan that will reduce both the overall tax burden and the political (and economic) costs of differentiated taxation.

## CONCLUSION

It may seem rather deflating to conclude a book calling for a return to true republicanism with a lesson on the need for prudence and a politics generally directed toward small, unspectacular victories. This was surely not the way of Thomas Paine. But it *was* the way of the statesmen who turned the passions aroused by Paine's *Common Sense* into the reason of a principled charter for a new nation. The first half of the Declaration's most famous paragraph declares the self-evident truths that justified resistance to the British crown and defines the purpose of the government that would replace it. The second half, beginning, in fact, with the word "prudence," carefully considers the conditions under which revolutionary action would not only be justified but also wise. Those who really care about life, liberty, and property cannot be indifferent to the ways in which all three of these are threatened and, in part, lost in a revolution itself. If the twenty-seven grievances appended to the end of the paragraph demonstrated the Founders' conclusion that there was no reasonable alternative to revolution, there is nothing in the whole of the document, despite the unusual urgency of the times, to suggest that the Founders believed themselves to be in any less need of practical wisdom in building our regime than we are in need of practical wisdom in recovering it.